Luke-Acts and
New Testament
Historiography

IBR Bibliographies

Tremper Longman III
General Editor and Old Testament Editor

Craig A. Evans
New Testament Editor

IBR Bibliographies No. 8

Luke-Acts and New Testament Historiography

Joel B. Green and Michael C. McKeever

Baker Books

A Division of Baker Book House Co
Grand Rapids, Michigan 49516

© 1994 by Joel B. Green and Michael C. McKeever

Published by Baker Books
a division of Baker Book House Company
P.O. Box 6287, Grand Rapids, MI 49516-6287

Printed in the United States of America

Library of Congress Cataloging-in-Publication Data

Green, Joel B., 1956–
    Luke-Acts and New Testament historiography / Joel B. Green and Michael C. McKeever.
      p. cm. — (IBR bibliographies ; no. 8)
    ISBN 0-8010-3872-3
    1. Bible. N.T. Luke—Abstracts. 2. Bible. N.T. Acts—Abstracts.
3. Bible. N.T. Luke—Historiography—Abstracts. 4. Bible. N.T. Acts—
Historiography—Abstracts. 5. History (Theology)—Biblical teaching—
Abstracts. I. McKeever, Michael C. II. Title. III. Series
BS2589.G74   1994
016.2264'06—dc20   94-40065

Contents

Series Preface

With the proliferation of journals and publishing houses dedicated to biblical studies, it has become difficult for even the most dedicated scholar to keep in touch with the vast materials now available for research in the different parts of the canon. How much more challenging for the minister, rabbi, student, or interested layperson! Herein lies the importance of bibliographies and in particular this series—IBR Bibliographies.

Bibliographies help direct students to works that are relevant to their research interests. Bibliographies cut down the time needed to locate materials, thus providing the researcher with more time to read, assimilate, and write. These benefits are especially true for the IBR Bibliographies. First, the series is conveniently laid out along the major divisions of the canon, with four volumes planned on the Old Testament, six on the New Testament, and four on methodology (see page 2). Each volume will contain approximately five hundred entries, arranged under various topics to allow for ease of reference. Since the possible entries far exceed this number, the compiler of each volume must select the more important and helpful works for inclusion. Furthermore, the entries are briefly annotated in order to inform the reader about their contents more specifically, once again giving guidance to the appropriate material and saving time by preventing the all too typical "wild goose chase" in the library.

One of the problems with published bibliographies in the past is that they are soon out of date. The development of computer-based publishing has changed this, however, and it is the plan of the Institute for Biblical Research and Baker Book House to publish updates of each volume about every five years.

Since the series is designed primarily for American and British students, the emphasis is on works written in English, with a five-percent limit on titles not translated into English. Fortunately, a number of the most important foreign-language works have been translated into English, and wherever this is the case this information is included along with the original publication data. Again keeping in mind the needs of the student, we have decided to list the English translation before the original title (for chronological purposes, the titles are arranged according to the dates of their original publication).

These bibliographies are presented under the sponsorship of the Institute for Biblical Research (IBR), an organization of evangelical Christian scholars with specialties in both Old and New Testaments and their ancillary disciplines. The IBR has met annually since 1970; its name and constitution were adopted in 1973. Besides its annual meetings (normally held the evening and morning prior to the annual meeting of the Society of Biblical Literature), the institute publishes a journal, *Bulletin for Biblical Research,* and conducts regional study groups on various biblical themes in several areas of the United States and Canada. The Institute for Biblical Research encourages and fosters scholarly research among its members, all of whom are at a level to qualify for a university lectureship. Finally, the IBR and the series editor extend their thanks to Baker Book House for its efforts to bring this series to publication. In particular, we would like to thank David Aiken for his wise guidance in giving shape to the project.

Tremper Longman III
Westminster Theological Seminary

Authors' Preface

In the last three decades, studies in the Gospel of Luke and the Acts of the Apostles have mushroomed. And in this century, Luke and Acts have been increasingly read as two parts of one larger work. This bibliography is an attempt to induct the student of Luke-Acts into this burgeoning field.

A further volume in the Institute for Biblical Research Bibliography series will address recent study of the Synoptic Gospels—Matthew, Mark, and Luke. Inevitably, there will be some overlap between these two volumes. Our attempt here, however, has been to focus on narrative, theology, genre, and historical issues embracing either Acts in particular or Luke and Acts together. Issues of a tradition-historical nature, for example, are left to the forthcoming volume on the Synoptic Gospels.

Luke-Acts and New Testament Historiography works within the boundaries of this series by focusing almost completely on materials published in English, and by limiting itself to some five hundred items. Persons desirous of more exhaustive bibliographical help may consult the materials in "1. Bibliographies, Surveys, and Histories of Research" (below).

We are grateful to the Flora Lamson Hewlett Library of the Graduate Theological Union, Berkeley, whose wide-ranging holdings and helpful staff have made this project much more manageable than might otherwise have been the case.

Joel B. Green
Michael C. McKeever
Advent 1993

Abbreviations

AMTBBB	Athenäum^S Monografien: Theologie; Bonner Biblische Beiträge
ANRW	*Aufstieg und Niedergang der Römischen Welt*
BETL	Bibliotheca Ephemeridum Theologicarum Lovaniensium
BJRL	*Bulletin of the John Rylands University Library of Manchester*
BTB	*Biblical Theology Bulletin*
CBQ	*Catholic Biblical Quarterly*
CTM	*Currents in Theology and Mission*
ExpTim	*Expository Times*
FRLANT	Forschungen zur Religion und Literatur des Alten und Neuen Testaments
Int	*Interpretation*
JBL	*Journal of Biblical Literature*
JSNT	*Journal for the Study of the New Testament*
JSNTSS	Journal for the Study of the New Testament Supplement Series
JTS	*Journal of Theological Studies*
NovT	*Novum Testamentum*
NovTSup	Novum Testamentum, Supplements
NTS	*New Testament Studies*
PRS	*Perspectives on Religious Studies*
SNTSMS	Society for New Testament Studies Monograph Series
TynB	*Tyndale Bulletin*
WUNT	Wissenschaftliche Untersuchungen zum Neuen Testament

Part 1

Luke-Acts

1

Bibliographies, Surveys, and Histories of Research

1 A. J. Mattill Jr. and M. B. Mattill. *A Classified Bibliography of Literature on the Acts of the Apostles*. New Testament Tools and Studies 7. Leiden: Brill, 1966.

   Some 6,650 entries organized under the following headings: textual, philological, literary, form-critical, historical, theological, and exegetical (i.e., on individual passages); covers literature through 1962.

2 W. C. van Unnik. "Luke-Acts: A Storm Center in Contemporary Scholarship." Pp. 15–32 in *Studies in Luke-Acts* (P. Schubert Festschrift). Edited by L. Keck and J. Martyn. Nashville: Abingdon, 1966. Reprinted in van Unnik's *Sparsa Collecta: The Collected Essays of W. C. van Unnik.* Part one: *Evangelia—Paulina—Acta*, pp. 92–110. NovTSup 29. Leiden: Brill, 1973.

   A critical survey of scholarship in the 1950s and '60s concerned with the transition from academic interest in Luke's sources and historiography to a concern with Luke as a theologian; van Unnik also urges further study of the place of Luke-Acts in early Christianity and against its Greco-Roman background, and its relation to the Old Testament and to early Christian writers.

3   W. W. Gasque. *A History of the Criticism of the Acts of the Apostles.* Beiträge zur Geschichte der biblischen Exegese 17. Tübingen: Mohr/Grand Rapids: Eerdmans, 1975. Second edition: Peabody, Mass.: Hendrickson, 1989.

A survey of the study of Acts, especially in the 19th and 20th centuries, underscoring the characterization of Luke as a theologian while affirming "the essential reliability of the narrative of Acts." The second edition includes the article mentioned in #9.

4   C. H. Talbert. "Shifting Sands: The Recent Study of the Gospel of Luke." *Int* 30 (1976): 381–95. Reprinted in *Interpreting the Gospels*, pp. 197–213. Edited by J. L. Mays. Philadelphia: Fortress, 1981.

Documents the transformation of Lukan studies from a particular concern with Luke as an historian and his use of sources to a greater focus on Luke as a theologian.

5   F. Bovon. *Luke the Theologian: Thirty-Three Years of Research (1950–83).* Translated by K. McKinney. Pittsburgh Theological Monograph Series 12. Allison Park, Pa.: Pickwick, 1987. Original title: *Luc le Théologien. Vingt-cinq ans de Recherches (1950–75).* Neuchâtel/Paris: Delachaux and Nestlé, 1978. Second edition: Genéve: Labor et Fides, 1988. The English translation contains an appendix, "Chronicles in Lucan Studies," originally published as "Chroniques du côté de chez Luc." *Revue théologie et de philosophie* 115 (1983): 175–89.

A series of thematic essays discussing Lukan scholarship from 1950–83, with extensive bibliographies on history and eschatology, the use of the Old Testament, christology, the Holy Spirit, salvation, discipleship, and the church.

6   G. Wagner (ed.). *An Exegetical Bibliography of the New Testament: Luke and Acts.* Macon, Ga.: Mercer University Press, 1985.

Arranged by section, pericope, and verse of the Gospel and Acts, with entries through 1981.

7   W. E. Mills. *A Bibliography of the Periodical Literature on the Acts of the Apostles 1962–1984.* NovTSup 58. Leiden: Brill, 1986.

An attempt to supplement #1 by listing almost 1,000 articles published in serials from 1962–88. Periodical, Scripture, and subject indices are provided.

8   P. F. Stuehrenberg. "The Study of Acts before the Reformation: A Bibliographic Introduction." *NovT* 29 (1987): 100–136.

Chronological listing of works by more than 140 authors before ca. 1520 which expressly or to some extent relate to Acts. Includes an author index and some annotations.

9   W. W. Gasque. "A Fruitful Field: Recent Study of the Acts of the Apostles." *Int* 42 (1988): 117–31. Reprinted in Gasque's *A History of the Criticism of the Acts of the Apostles,* pp. 345–59. Second edition: Peabody, Mass.: Hendrickson, 1989.

A survey of study of Acts, especially in the 1970s and '80s, concentrating on the purpose, structure, and theology of Acts; a section on "areas for further study" is included.

10   I. H. Marshall. "The Present State of Lucan Studies." *Themelios* 14 (1989): 52–57. Reprinted in revised form as a postscript in Marshall's *Luke: Historian and Theologian,* pp. 223–35. Second edition: Grand Rapids: Zondervan, 1989.

Assesses Lukan scholarship since 1979, focusing especially on the twin issues, history and theology.

11   M. A. Powell. *What Are They Saying about Luke?* New York/Mahwah: Paulist, 1989.

An excellent, panoramic introduction to the contemporary study of the Gospel of Luke.

12   F. Van Segbroeck. *The Gospel of Luke: A Cumulative Bibliography (1973–1988).* BETL 88. Leuven: Leuven University Press, 1989.

Lists almost 2,800 Lukan studies during the 15-year period ending in 1988, then provides a series of thematic (on a range of literary and theological issues) and verse-by-verse indices.

13   M. A. Powell. *What Are They Saying about Acts?* New York/Mahwah: Paulist, 1991.

An excellent, panoramic introduction to the contemporary study of the Acts of the Apostles.

14   I. H. Marshall. *The Acts of the Apostles.* New Testament Guides. Sheffield: JSOT Press, 1992.

A concise examination of recent study of Acts, beginning with literary questions, then moving to theological issues, historical matters, and finally to brief discussion of the book's contemporary relevance.

15   M. C. Parsons and J. B. Tyson (eds.). *Cadbury, Knox, and Talbert: American Contributions to the Study of Acts.* Atlanta: Scholars Press, 1992.

A collection of essays exploring the contribution of these three North Americans to the study of Acts spanning the twentieth century. D. L. Tiede concludes this symposium with an essay on the future of the study of Luke-Acts.

2

Commentaries on the Gospel of Luke and the Acts of the Apostles

2.1 The Gospel of Luke

16 A. Plummer. *A Critical and Exegetical Commentary on the Gospel According to S. Luke.* International Critical Commentary. Edinburgh: T. & T. Clark, 1896.

Though dated in many respects, this remains a classic discussion of the Third Gospel, especially on issues of language and style.

17 F. W. Danker. *Jesus and the New Age According to St. Luke: A Commentary on the Third Gospel.* St. Louis: Clayton, 1972. Second edition: *Jesus and the New Age: A Commentary on St. Luke's Gospel.* Philadelphia: Fortress, 1988.

A commentary on the Gospel of Luke as a coherent literary work with particular attention to the possibilities of Luke's reception in a Greco-Roman cultural environment.

18 I. H. Marshall. *The Gospel of Luke: A Commentary on the Greek Text.* New International Greek Testament Commentary. Grand Rapids: Eerdmans, 1978.

A commentary on the Greek text of Luke, emphasizing historical- and redaction-critical issues.

19   J. A. Fitzmyer. *The Gospel According to Luke: Introduction, Translation, and Notes.* 2 vols. Anchor Bible 28–28A. Garden City, N.Y.: Doubleday, 1981/85.

A massive commentary from a tradition-critical approach, also providing a history of recent research on each pericope.

20   C. H. Talbert. *Reading Luke: A Literary and Theological Commentary on the Third Gospel.* New York: Crossroad, 1982.

A relatively brief commentary focusing on the shape of the final text rather than on questions of sources or traditions.

21   M. D. Goulder. *Luke: A New Paradigm.* 2 vols. JSNTSS 20. Sheffield: JSOT, 1989.

An attempt to reorient understanding of Luke around a nontraditional answer to the question of Luke's sources. For Goulder, Luke wrote his Gospel by combining Mark and Matthew; other material derives from Lukan creativity.

22   J. Nolland. *Luke.* 3 vols. Word Biblical Commentary 35. Dallas: Word, 1989–93.

A reading of the Third Gospel understood ". . . as an exercise in communication, deliberately undertaken by the Gospel writer with at least some focused sense of the actual or potential needs of his audience" (xii).

23   C. F. Evans. *Saint Luke.* Trinity Press International New Testament Commentary. London: SCM/Philadelphia: Trinity, 1990.

A pericope-by-pericope discussion of the Gospel, sometimes more theological in orientation, sometimes more historical and tradition-critical.

24   L. T. Johnson. *The Gospel of Luke.* Sacra Pagina 3. Collegeville, Minn.: Liturgical, 1991.

A literary analysis of the Third Gospel, concerned with ". . . what Luke is saying and how he goes about saying it" (xii).

25 R. H. Stein. *Luke.* New American Commentary 24. Nashville: Broadman, 1991.

An exploration of how Luke has interpreted the historical traditions constitutive of his Gospel; what is Luke trying "to teach" in each passage?

26 D. L. Bock. *Luke*, vol. 1: *1:1–9:50.* Baker Exegetical Commentary on the New Testament 3. Grand Rapids: Baker, 1994.

The first of a projected two-volume, verse-by-verse study of the Third Gospel, the particular focus of which is historical (including questions of historical veracity, historical background, sources, form criticism, and redaction criticism) and exegetical.

2.2 The Acts of the Apostles

27 F. F. Bruce. *The Acts of the Apostles: The Greek Text with Introduction and Commentary.* London: Tyndale/Grand Rapids: Eerdmans, 1951. Second edition: 1952. Third revised and enlarged edition: Leicester: InterVarsity (Apollos)/Grand Rapids: Eerdmans, 1990.

A verse-by-verse discussion of philological, grammatical, and historical features of the Greek text.

28 F. F. Bruce. *The Book of the Acts.* New International Commentary on the New Testament. London: Marshall, Morgan & Scott/Grand Rapids: Eerdmans, 1954. Revised edition: Grand Rapids: Eerdmans, 1988.

A verse-by-verse exposition, whose special concern is with the historical background of the events narrated in Acts.

29 E. Haenchen. *The Acts of the Apostles: A Commentary.* Oxford: Blackwell/Philadelphia: Westminster, 1971. Translated by B. Noble and G. Shinn under the supervision of H. Anderson, with the translation revised by R. McL. Wilson. Original title: *Die Apostelgeschichte.* Kritisch-exegetischer Kommentar über das Neue Testament. 14th ed. Göttingen: Vandenhoeck & Ruprecht, 1965.

Though somewhat dated, still the major critical commentary on Acts, concerned above all with the theological agenda of the Book of Acts—an agenda which, Haenchen argues, overrides any Lukan considerations of historicity.

30 H. Conzelmann. *The Acts of the Apostles: A Commentary on the Acts of the Apostles.* Translated by J. Limburg et al. Philadelphia: Fortress, 1987. Original title: *Die Apostelgeschichte.* 2d ed. Handbuch zum Neuen Testament 7. Tübingen: Mohr, 1972.

Although only recently available in English, this critical and historical commentary is already dated (though with updated bibliographies); verse-by-verse format.

31 I. H. Marshall. *The Acts of the Apostles: An Introduction and Commentary.* Tyndale New Testament Commentary. Leicester: InterVarsity/Grand Rapids: Eerdmans, 1980.

Though limited in scope by the purpose of the series in which it is published, this commentary is a serviceable companion to Haenchen (#29), emphasizing as it does Luke's theological *and* historical commitments.

32 L. T. Johnson. *The Acts of the Apostles.* Sacra Pagina 5. Collegeville, Minn.: Liturgical, 1992.

Treating Acts as apologetic history, this commentary focuses above all on Luke's literary artistry and historiographical interests.

33 J. B. Polhill. *Acts.* New American Commentary 26. Nashville: Broadman, 1992.

An exposition written for pastors and students, concerned with both the theological and historical significance of Acts.

3

Classic and Contemporary Approaches to Luke-Acts

Gospels-research prior to World War II centered especially on the quest of the historical Jesus and the growth of the Synoptic tradition. Because under almost any reckoning (i.e., whether according to the at-the-time almost universally held theory of Markan priority or the scarcely mentioned hypothesis of Matthean priority) Luke was deemed secondary, the Third Gospel *as a Gospel* received little attention in special studies. The early work of H. J. Cadbury marks a significant exception to this lacuna outside the commentaries. Acts-studies, on the other hand, was spotlighted for its importance in understanding the historical development of the beginnings of Christianity. Landmark studies by Dibelius on Acts (#36) and Conzelmann on Luke (#37) set the agenda for the modern study of these two books by raising questions of Luke's literary and theological program. More recently, the ensuing redaction-critical study of Luke-Acts has been supplemented—and in some areas, superseded—by social-scientific, literary, and canon-critical approaches. To date, the old and the new have not so much been integrated as that the older concerns have been displaced by the newer—with one important exception, the continuation of the study of the historical character of Acts and the historical veracity of the events it narrates (see below, chapter 10).

3.1 Classic Studies of Luke-Acts

34   F. J. Foakes-Jackson and K. Lake (eds.). *The Beginnings of Christianity.* Part one: *The Acts of the Apostles.* 5 vols. London: Macmillan, 1922–33. Reprinted Grand Rapids: Baker, 1979.

A collection of studies on "Jewish, Gentile, and Christian Backgrounds" (vol. 1); introductory material related to the composition, purpose, and author of Acts, together with a history of the criticism of Acts (vol. 2); an examination of the text of Acts (vol. 3); a translation and commentary on Acts (vol. 4); and a variety of theological and historical issues raised by a study of Acts (vol. 5).

35   H. J. Cadbury. *The Making of Luke-Acts.* London: Macmillan, 1927. Second edition: London: SPCK, 1968.

A comprehensive exploration of the literary process and rhetorical concerns leading to the production of Luke-Acts.

36   M. Dibelius. *Studies in the Acts of the Apostles.* Edited by H. Greeven. Translated by M. Ling. London: SCM/New York: Charles Scribner's Sons, 1956. Original title: *Aufsätze zur Apostelgeschichte.* FRLANT 60. Göttingen: Vandenhoeck & Ruprecht, 1951. Second edition: 1953.

Dibelius' essays collected here, most of them appearing first from 1923–49, set the stage for the modern, critical study of Acts.

37   H. Conzelmann. *The Theology of St. Luke.* Translated by G. Buswell. London: Faber & Faber/New York: Harper & Row, 1960. Reprinted London: SCM, 1982. Original title: *Die Mitte der Zeit.* Tübingen: Mohr, 1953. Second edition: 1957.

The ground-breaking redaction-critical study of Luke, from which much subsequent study of Lukan theology has taken its starting point. Although many of Conzelmann's ideas are disputed (e.g., the periodization of salvation history, Luke's "early catholicism," Luke's interest in and knowledge of Palestinian geography, etc.), he nevertheless drew attention to key aspects of Lukan thought deserving exploration.

38 L. E. Keck and J. L. Martyn (eds.). *Studies in Luke-Acts* (P. Schubert Festschrift). Nashville: Abingdon, 1966.

This collection bears witness to the importance of locating Luke-Acts in the development of early Christian history. Includes essays by W. C. van Unnik, H. J. Cadbury, H. Conzelmann, E. Haenchen, J. Knox, et al.

3.2 Luke-Acts and the Social Sciences

Turn-of-the-century historical-critical research largely turned away from a primary interest in the socio-historical milieu within which the New Testament materials were written, in favor of a history-of-religions approach and a search for the ever-elusive "what actually happened." The growth of social-scientific research in the last two decades has begun to redress this balance, though such investigations have only of late turned their attention to Luke and Acts. These approaches have drawn on comparative anthropology and social-scientific models for laying bare the fabric of Luke's social world. See D. M. May, *Social Scientific Criticism of the New Testament: A Bibliography*, pp. 46–48. National Association of Baptist Professors Bibliographic Series 4. Macon, Ga.: Mercer University Press, 1991.

39 H. J. Cadbury. *The Book of Acts in History*. New York: Harper/London: A. & C. Black, 1955.

An exploration of the social history of the larger world in which the narrative of Acts is set.

40 P. F. Esler. *Community and Gospel in Luke-Acts: The Social and Political Motivations of Lucan Theology.* SNTSMS 57. Cambridge: Cambridge University Press, 1987.

Employing a method that combines redaction-critical and social-scientific approaches, Esler argues that, working from his perspective toward the end of the first century C.E., Luke's purpose was to rewrite the history of the church so as to help the Christian community legitimate itself over against Judaism.

41 H. Moxnes. *The Economy of the Kingdom: Social Conflict and Economic Relations in Luke's Gospel.* Overtures to Biblical Theology. Philadelphia: Fortress, 1988.

Integrating cultural anthropological studies with compositional and redaction-critical approaches to the Third Gospel, Moxnes portrays the social world of the Gospel of Luke in which the Evangelist's concerns with social and economic issues find their meaning.

42   J. H. Neyrey (ed.). *The Social World of Luke-Acts: Models for Interpretation*. Peabody, Mass.: Hendrickson, 1991.

This collection of essays aims "to produce a comprehensive volume of Luke-Acts studies that might serve as a representative collection of materials and models needed for understanding biblical texts within the cultures of the people who produced them" (p. x). Contributors include J. H. Neyrey, B. J. Malina, R. L. Rohrbaugh, D. E. Oakman, J. J. Pilch, J. H. Elliott, H. Moxnes, V. K. Robbins, and M. McVann.

43   B. J. Malina and R. L. Rohrbaugh. *Social-Science Commentary on the Synoptic Gospels*, pp. 279–413. Minneapolis: Fortress, 1992.

Provides comments on the cultural world assumed to have been presupposed by the written text of the Gospel of Luke.

3.3 Luke-Acts in Literary and Canonical Perspective

Although the *genre* of Luke and Acts remains a matter of debate, there is now a widespread recognition that in these volumes one faces a narrative susceptible to investigation by means of newer literary and narratological approaches. In large part, this avenue of study grows out of an increased commitment to the perspective that Luke is doing more than simply gathering together a collection of disparate traditions, but is in these volumes shaping a self-conscious, purposeful narrative account of the ministry of Jesus and its continuation in the early church.

44   R. C. Tannehill. *The Narrative Unity of Luke-Acts: A Literary Interpretation*. 2 vols. Foundations and Facets. Philadelphia: Fortress, 1986, 1990.

Claiming that Luke-Acts constitutes a narrative unity, that Luke's story is "constructed to influence its readers or hearers," and that "there are particular literary techniques used for this purpose," Tannehill explores Luke's "narrative rhetoric" (vol. 2, p. 4). Volume one examines "narrative roles" in Luke; volume two follows the text of Acts in a more traditional way from beginning to end.

45 M. C. Parsons. *The Departure of Jesus in Luke-Acts: The Ascension Narratives in Context.* JSNTSS 21. Sheffield: JSOT Press, 1987.

Applies both tradition-critical and more recent literary approaches to the ascension narratives in Luke 24 and Acts 1.

46 R. W. Wall. "The Acts of the Apostles in Canonical Context." *BTB* 18 (1988): 16–24. Reprinted in R. W. Wall and E. E. Lemcio, *The New Testament as Canon: A Reader in Canonical Criticism*, pp. 110–28. JSNTSS 76. Sheffield: JSOT Press, 1992.

Proposes that the hermeneutical key for contemporary reading of Acts shift from a focus on the historical relation of Luke and Acts to its canonical position between the Gospels and Letters.

47 R. L. Brawley. *Centering on God: Method and Message in Luke-Acts.* Literary Currents in Biblical Interpretation. Louisville: Westminster/John Knox, 1990.

Employing a wide array of newer literary methods, Brawley explores how Luke-Acts can be interpreted so as to include in its message modern believers.

48 J. D. Kingsbury. *Conflict in Luke: Jesus, Authorities, Disciples.* Minneapolis: Fortress, 1991.

Following an introduction to central concerns of narrative criticism, Kingsbury reads the Gospel of Luke through three story lines—that of Jesus, that of the Jewish authorities, and that of the disciples.

49 J. A. Darr. *On Character Building: The Reader and the Rhetoric of Characterization in Luke-Acts.* Literary Currents in Biblical Interpretation. Louisville: Westminster/John Knox, 1992.

An exploration of how the Lukan text and its reader cooperate to construct understandings of characters within the narrative; this process is illustrated with reference to John the Baptist, the Pharisees, and Herod the Tetrarch.

50   S. M. Sheeley. *Narrative Asides in Luke-Acts.* JSNTSS 72. Sheffield: JSOT Press, 1992.

A narrative analysis of how Luke speaks directly to the reader in his narrative, so as to draw the reader more fully into his confidence and into the world of the narrative.

51   W. S. Kurz. *Reading Luke-Acts: Dynamics of Biblical Narrative.* Louisville: Westminster/John Knox, 1993.

Although cognizant and appreciative of the status of Luke-Acts as historical and theological documents, Kurz affirms their primary status as *narratives,* and as books within the Christian Bible. This leads to a circumspect use of contemporary literary approaches and the launching of a canonical reading of Luke-Acts.

4

The Genre, Unity, and Purpose
of Luke-Acts

Up until the most recent chapter in Lukan studies, the *unity* of Luke-Acts was almost universally assumed, even if diverse viewpoints on its genre and purpose continued to vie for support. Even this point of agreement has begun to attract dissenting voices, however. Central in these various discussions is the role of the preface of Luke (1:1–4) and its relation to the opening of Acts.

4.1 The Prefaces in Luke-Acts

Is Luke 1:1–4 the preface to Luke-Acts or to the Gospel of Luke only? This, as well as the role of the preface in identifying the genre and purpose of Luke's literary project, has been at the heart of the discussion of Luke 1:1–4. In addition, the preface has begun to be examined for the insight it might shed on the social location of its author and implied audience.

52 H. J. Cadbury. "Commentary on the Preface of Luke." Pp. 489–510 in *The Beginnings of Christianity*, part 1: *The Acts of the Apostles*, ed. F. J. Foakes-Jackson and K. Lake, Vol. 2: *Prolegomena—II: Criticism.* London: Macmillan, 1922.

A word-by-word analysis of Luke 1:1–4, taken as a preface to Luke and Acts, in the light of contemporary Hellenistic literature.

53   D. Earl. "Prologue-form in Ancient Historiography." *ANRW* 1.2:842–56 (1972).

Discusses the rules observed by Greek and Latin historiographers for an opening sentence or paragraph—including: setting forth the subject, its importance and implications, and minor variations as to the inclusion and position of the author's name.

54   W. C. van Unnik. "Once More St. Luke's Prologue." *Neotestamentica* 7 (1973): 7–26.

A detailed examination of the Lukan prologue against the background of ideas current among historians in antiquity demonstrates Luke's purpose: ". . . to make known the truth of the Christian message" by providing "historical evidence which was unimpeachable by the standards of his time" (19).

55   I. I. Du Plessis. "Once More: The Purpose of Luke's Prologue (Lk 1:1–4)." *NovT* 16 (1974): 259–71.

Luke made use of the conventional form and vocabulary of other Greek authors, but adapted these so as to introduce his own agenda—namely, ". . . to serve Christianity with a true report of *God acting in history*" (p. 271).

56   V. K. Robbins. "Prefaces in Greco-Roman Biography and Luke-Acts." Vol. 2, pp. 193–207 in *Society of Biblical Literature 1978 Seminar Papers*. 2 vols. Edited by P. J. Achtemeier. Missoula, Mont.: Scholars Press, 1978. Reprinted in *PRS* 6 (1979): 94–108.

The prefaces in Luke and Acts manifest features common to Hellenistic biography—specifically, didactic biography; Luke has employed this genre to mount a defense of Christianity.

57   R. J. Dillon. "Previewing Luke's Project from His Prologue (Luke 1:1–4)." *CBQ* 43 (1981): 205–27.

A comprehensive discussion of Luke's preface from the perspective of how the narrative of Luke-Acts develops subsequent to its prologue; argues that the "certainty"

Luke attempted to provide derived from the connection between the sacred history of promise-fulfillment and the contemporary situation of Christian belief.

58 T. Callen. "The Preface of Luke-Acts and Historiography." *NTS* 31 (1985): 576–81.

Luke's preface marks his work as belonging to the genre of historiography; its statement of purpose identifies it further as belonging to that historiography concerned with providing a true account of something.

59 L. C. A. Alexander. "Luke's Preface in the Context of Greek Preface-Writing." *NovT* 28 (1986): 48–74.

Luke's preface is akin to those of the "scientific tradition" (e.g., engineering, medicine) and this has implications for our understanding of his *audience* and the *genre* of his work.

60 R. R. Creech. "The Most Excellent Narratee: The Significance of Theophilus in Luke-Acts." Pp. 107–26 in *With Steadfast Purpose: Essays on Acts in Honor of Henry Jackson Flanders Jr.* Edited by N. H. Keathley. Waco, Tex.: Baylor University Press, 1990.

Employing a narratological analysis of Theophilus as the narratee of Luke-Acts, Creech concludes that Theophilus is ". . . a God-fearing Gentile being asked to consider Christianity" (p. 126).

61 F. Ó Fearghail. *The Introduction to Luke-Acts: A Study of the Role of Luke 1,1–4,44 in the Composition of Luke's Two-Volume Work* (esp. pp. 85–116). Analecta Biblica 126. Rome: Pontifical Biblical Institute Press, 1991.

Explores Luke 1:1–4 within the larger section, 1:1–4:44, arguing that Luke is writing "kerygmatic history."

62 D. P. Moessner. "The Meaning of ΚΑΘΕΞΗΣ in the Lukan Prologue as a Key to the Distinctive Contribution of Luke's Narrative among the 'Many.'" Vol. 2, pp. 1513–28 in *The Four Gospels 1992: Festschrift Frans Neirynck.* Edited by F. Van Segbroeck. BETL 100. Leuven: Leuven University Press, 1992.

"To read Luke's two-volumes καθεξῆς [in order] is to 'get his story straight!'—'to gain a firmer grasp of the true sig-

nificance of those events of which you have been in-
structed' (Lk 1,4)" (p. 1528).

63   L. C. A. Alexander. *The Preface to Luke's Gospel: Literary
         Convention and Social Context in Luke 1.1–4 and Acts 1.1.*
         SNTSMS 78. Cambridge: Cambridge University Press,
         1993.

         An examination of the literary background of the prefaces
         of Luke and Acts indicates that their closest parallels are
         located in Greek scientific and technical manuals of the
         classical and Roman eras. The repercussions of this find-
         ing for our understanding of the genre of Luke and Acts
         and the social context of the author and his first readers
         are then explored.

64   H. Riley. *Preface to Luke.* Macon, Ga.: Mercer University,
         1993.

         Working from the assumption that Luke was based on an
         early version of Matthew and was written by Luke, the
         sometime companion of Paul, at a correspondingly early
         date, Riley traces the implications of Luke's preface for is-
         sues including sources, traditions, authorship, and audi-
         ence.

4.2 The Genre of Luke-Acts

Particularly because of its content and the prefaces of Luke's
work, Acts has long been understood as the first example of
Christian historiography. Questions about the historical veracity
of the Acts account and ongoing assessment of Acts within the
context of the literature of Jewish and Greco-Roman antiquity
have opened this identification of genre to lively discussion. Today, Acts has been located within all of the three primary genres
of the Roman world—historiography, the novel, and the biography. Now moving to the forefront of this discussion is the related
matter of whether Luke and Acts of necessity belong to the same
genre. See §§4.1, 4.3.

65   C. H. Talbert. *Literary Patterns, Theological Themes, and
         the Genre of Luke-Acts.* Society of Biblical Literature Mono-
         graph Series 20. Missoula, Mont.: Scholars Press, 1974.

Luke-Acts is a biographical succession narrative, both oc-
casional in nature (like Paul's letters) and carefully
planned compositionally.

66   C. H. Talbert. *What Is a Gospel? The Genre of the Canonical Gospels.* Philadelphia: Fortress, 1977.

Continues the discussion of #65, and reaches the same
conclusion.

67   S. P. Schierling and M. J. Schierling. "The Influence of the
Ancient Romances on Acts of the Apostles." *Classical Bulletin* 54 (1978): 81–88.

Though Acts shares a significant number of genre features with ancient romances, the genre features which it
lacks preclude its being classified as such.

68   S. M. Praeder. "Luke-Acts and the Ancient Novel." Pp.
269–92 in *Society of Biblical Literature 1981 Seminar Papers.* Edited by K. H. Richards. Chico, Calif.: Scholars Press,
1981.

Employing a narrative approach to the study of Luke-
Acts, Praeder identifies Luke-Acts as an ancient novel in
genre and a Christian ancient novel in subgenre.

69   D. L. Barr and J. L. Wentling. "The Convention of Classical
Biography and the Genre of Luke-Acts: A Preliminary
Study." Pp. 63–88 in *Luke-Acts: New Perspectives from the
Society of Biblical Literature Seminar.* Edited by C. H. Tal-
bert. New York: Crossroad, 1984.

Although first-century readers might not have understood Luke-Acts as a biography *per se,* they would have
read it with expectations raised by their recognition of its
important similarities to the biographical genre.

70   D. E. Aune. *The New Testament in Its Literary Environment,* pp. 77–157. Library of Early Christianity 8. Philadelphia: Westminster, 1987.

Sets Luke-Acts within the larger context of Hellenistic,
Israelite, and Jewish historiography, concluding that
"Luke was an eclectic Hellenistic Christian who narrated
the early history of Christianity from its origins in Judaism with Jesus of Nazareth through its emergence as a rel-

atively independent religious movement open to all ethnic groups" (pp. 138–39); this qualifies Luke-Acts as belonging to the genre of "general history."

71   R. I. Pervo. *Profit with Delight: The Literary Genre of the Acts of the Apostles*. Philadelphia: Fortress, 1987.

Argues that Acts is an edifying historical novel.

72   R. I. Pervo. "Must Luke and Acts Belong to the Same Genre?" Pp. 309–16 in *Society of Biblical Literature 1989 Seminar Papers*. Edited by D. J. Lull. Atlanta: Scholars Press, 1989.

Argues that the unity of Luke and Acts at the level of genre has been more presumed than demonstrated with reference to models of genre in antiquity.

73   D. L. Balch. "The Genre of Luke-Acts: Individual Biography, Adventure Novel, or Political History?" *Southwestern Journal of Theology* 33 (1990): 5–19.

Critically reviews #65, #66, and #71, then develops the case that Luke-Acts is "ancient history" by comparing Luke's work with significant features of Dionysius' *Roman Antiquities*.

74   P. L. Shuler. "The Genre(s) of the Gospels." Pp. 459–83 in *The Interrelations of the Gospels*. Edited by D. L. Dungan. BETL 95. Leuven: Leuven University Press, 1990.

Taken on its own, the Third Gospel belongs to the category of encomium biographical literature; taken together, "Luke-Acts confronts the reader with an encomiastically charged account of Jesus-church to which the proper response is faith-participation" (p. 479).

75   P. Stuhlmacher. "The Genre(s) of the Gospels: Response to P. L. Shuler." Pp. 484–94 in *The Interrelations of the Gospels*. Edited by D. L. Dungan. BETL 95. Leuven: Leuven University Press, 1990.

Contra #74, the prefaces to Luke and Acts suggest that the Gospel is a (reliable) historical narrative—to be distinguished from the Hellenistic biography, for which history played little or no role at all.

76 R. A. Burridge. *What Are the Gospels? A Comparison with Graeco-Roman Biography.* SNTSMS 70. Cambridge: Cambridge University Press, 1992.

After segregating Luke and Acts as necessarily belonging to one genre, Burridge argues that the Third Gospel belongs to the genre of Greco-Roman biography while the generic features of historiography, romance, and the monograph begin to appear in Acts.

77 D. W. Palmer. "Acts and the Historical Monograph." *TynB* 43 (1992): 373–88.

Luke and Acts are not necessarily related in terms of genre, and Acts is best understood as a historical writing treating a limited issue or period of time (cf. Palmer's essay in #372).

78 G. L. Sterling. *Historiography and Self-Definition: Josephus, Luke-Acts and Apologetic Historiography.* NovTSup 64. Leiden: Brill, 1992.

Argues that Acts belongs to a type of history whose narratives "relate the story of a particular people by deliberating hellenizing their native traditions" (p. 374).

4.3 The Unity and Purpose of Luke-Acts

Earlier attempts to grapple with the character of the Acts of the Apostles as an apology for Paul faltered as Luke and Acts began more and more to be understood as two parts of a single work. How might the Gospel of Luke and the first half of Acts be subsumed under that narrow statement of purpose? The role of the prefaces in interpreting the purpose of Luke-Acts (see §4.1) and the question of the genre or genres of Luke and Acts (see §4.2) have also been examined carefully for their input on the question of purpose. Other data have been moved into the discussion too, including the often-noticed parallels between Luke and Acts and, more recently, information about the concerns of Luke and his implied audience that can be garnered from within the narrative. And the degree to which Luke can be regarded as promoting friendly relations between church and empire, a staple of the discussion in previous decades, has been countered repeatedly.

Clearly, how one judges the purpose of Luke's work is intimately related to how one judges the issue of the unity of Luke-Acts.

79   W. C. van Unnik. "Remarks on the Purpose of Luke's Historical Writing." Pp. 6–15 in *Sparsa Collecta: The Collected Essays of W. C. van Unnik*. Part one: *Evangelia—Paulina—Acta*, pp. 92–110. NovTSup 29. Leiden: Brill, 1973. Original title: "Opmerkingen over het doel van Lucas' Geschiedwerk (Luc. 1.4)." *Nederlands Theologisch Tijdschrift* 9 (1955): 332–31.
   Luke's two volumes must be read together; their purpose is not only to preach, but also to bring to his readers "complete certainty" regarding Jesus' work of salvation.

80   W. C. van Unnik. "The 'Book of Acts': The Confirmation of the Gospel." *NovT* 4 (1960): 26–59. Reprinted in *Sparsa Collecta: The Collected Essays of W. C. van Unnik*. Part one: *Evangelia—Paulina—Acta*, pp. 340–73. NovTSup 29. Leiden: Brill, 1973.
   God's plan of salvation is set forth in Luke, and Acts confirms its truth and relevance for those living after the earthly ministry of Jesus.

81   C. H. Talbert. *Luke and the Gnostics: An Examination of the Lucan Purpose*. Nashville: Abingdon, 1966.
   Luke-Acts was written to serve as a defense against Gnosticism.

82   A. J. Mattill Jr. "The Purpose of Acts: Schneckenburger Reconsidered." Pp. 108–22 in *Apostolic History and the Gospel: Biblical and Historical Essays Presented to F. F. Bruce on His 60th Birthday*. Edited by W. W. Gasque and R. P. Martin. Exeter: Paternoster/Grand Rapids: Eerdmans, 1970.
   Acts was written as "a defense of the Apostle [Paul] of the Gentiles against Jewish-Christian charges originating chiefly in Jerusalem and Rome" (p. 122).

83   A. J. Mattill Jr. "*Naherwartung, Fernerwartung*, and the Purpose of Luke-Acts: Weymouth Reconsidered." *CBQ* 34 (1972): 276–93.
   Contra those who see no imminent eschatology in Acts, Mattill argues that Luke's purpose was to provide an apol-

ogy for Paul, not to write a history for future generations of Christians; Luke's purpose was to defend and facilitate the spread of the gospel and, thus, to expedite the apocalyptic plan. (See #247.)

84 P. S. Minear. "Dear Theo: The Kerygmatic Intention and Claim of the Book of Acts." *Int* 27 (1973): 131–50.

A purpose of Luke was to reinforce trust in the power of God's word through his mediation of an encounter between "eyewitnesses and ministers of the word" (Luke 1:1–4) and his audience.

85 R. F. O'Toole. "Why Did Luke Write Acts (Lk-Acts)?" *BTB* 7 (1977): 66–76.

A critical survey of prior attempts to ascertain the Lukan purpose based on two criteria: (1) the successful theory(ies) must be based on the text of Luke-Acts and (2) the significance of a proposed aim for Acts must be measured against the degree to which it makes sense of both Lukan volumes.

86 A. J. Mattill Jr. "The Date and Purpose of Luke-Acts: Rackham Reconsidered." *CBQ* 40 (1978): 335–50.

Presents an argument for a pre–70 c.e. date of Acts, then explores the corollaries of that date for the authorship and purpose of Acts.

87 K. P. Donfried. "Attempts at Understanding the Purpose of Luke-Acts: Christology and the Salvation of the Gentiles." Pp. 112–22 in *Christological Perspectives: Essays in Honor of Harvey K. McArthur*. Edited by R. F. Berkey and S. A. Edwards. New York: Pilgrim, 1982.

Luke is attempting to demonstrate the legitimacy of the Gentile mission for his predominantly Jewish Christian audience.

88 R. Maddox. *The Purpose of Luke-Acts*. Studies of the New Testament in Its World. Edinburgh: T. & T. Clark/FRLANT; Göttingen: Vandenhoeck & Ruprecht, 1982.

Luke wrote to reassure an increasingly Gentile church of the validity of its faith in spite of Jewish rejection of Jesus and the gospel.

89   R. F. O'Toole. "Parallels between Jesus and His Disciples in Luke-Acts: A Further Study." *Biblische Zeitschrift* 27 (1983): 195–212.

An examination of the parallels between Jesus and his disciples leads to the conclusion "that Luke's main aim in these parallels was to establish a continuity between Luke-Acts"; secondary reasons might include an apology for Paul, the imitation of Christ, and to address the problem of the delay of the parousia (p. 212).

90   I. H. Marshall. "Luke and His 'Gospel.'" Pp. 289–308 in *Das Evangelium und die Evangelien: Vortäge vom Tübinger Symposium 1982*. Edited by P. Stuhlmacher. WUNT 28. Tübingen: Mohr, 1983. Reprinted in *The Gospel and the Gospels*, pp. 273–92. Edited by P. Stuhlmacher. Grand Rapids: Eerdmans, 1991.

"Luke's main purpose was to confirm the kerygma/catechetical instruction heard by people like Theophilus with a fuller account of the basis of the kerygma in the story of Jesus, as handed down by faithful witnesses, and in the continuing story of the way in which, through the activity of the witnesses, the church, composed of Jews and Gentiles, came into existence" (p. 307) (see Marshall's essay in #372).

91   P. W. Walaskay. *"And so we came to Rome": The Political Perspective of St. Luke*. SNTSMS 49. Cambridge: Cambridge University Press, 1983.

Luke's aim was to provide an apology to the Christian church on behalf of the Roman empire.

92   S. M. Praeder. "Jesus-Paul, Peter-Paul, and Jesus-Peter Parallels in Luke-Acts: A History of Reader Response." Pp. 23–39 in *Society of Biblical Literature 1984 Seminar Papers*. Edited by K. H. Richards. Chico, Calif.: Scholars Press, 1984.

Surveys attempts to locate and interpret parallels in Luke-Acts over the past two centuries, and calls for greater methodological self-criticism in such analyses.

93   F. F. Bruce. "Paul's Apologetic and the Purpose of Acts." *BJRL* 69 (1986–87): 379–93.

Acts addresses charges of subversive activity raised against Paul and Christians in general, to commend the Christian church to the favorable attention of Rome.

94   R. J. Cassidy. *Society and Politics in the Acts of the Apostles*. Maryknoll, N.Y.: Orbis, 1987.

Building on his similar analysis of the Third Gospel (#268), Cassidy argues against any notion that the purpose of Acts was to provide a political apologetic—either for Rome or for the church. Instead, Luke wrote to encourage among his Christian audience a fundamental allegiance to Jesus which called for a basic social and political stance within the empire.

95   P. F. Esler. *Community and Gospel in Luke-Acts: The Social and Political Motivations of Lucan Theology.* SNTSMS 57. Cambridge: Cambridge University Press, 1987.

Luke's purpose was to rewrite the history of the church so as to help the Christian community legitimate itself over against Judaism.

96   J. M. Dawsey. "The Literary Unity of Luke-Acts: Questions of Style—a Task for Literary Critics." *NTS* 35 (1989): 48–66.

A close reading of the style of the Greek text of the Third Gospel and the Acts of the Apostles raises questions about the literary unity of these two volumes.

97   M. C. Parsons. "The Unity of Luke-Acts: Rethinking the *Opinio Communic.*" Pp. 29–53 in *With Steadfast Purpose: Essays on Acts in Honor of Henry Jackson Flanders Jr.* Edited by N. H. Keathley. Waco, Tex.: Baylor University Press, 1990.

A programmatic essay allowing for theological coherence between Luke and Acts, but arguing against the unity of Luke and Acts with respect to genre and narrative purpose.

98   M. C. Parsons and R. I. Pervo. *Rethinking the Unity of Luke and Acts.* Minneapolis: Fortress, 1993.

Argues that the unity of Luke-Acts has been assumed more than argued, then examines the possible *generic, narrative,* and *theological* unity of Luke and Acts. Concludes that Luke and Acts are each complete in themselves, with Acts a sequel to Luke.

5

The Theology of Luke-Acts

5.1 Symposia and General Discussions of Lukan Theology

Only within the last half of this century have New Testament scholars begun to recognize Luke as a theologian in his own right. Foundational in this regard were the works of Dibelius (#36) and Conzelmann (#37) which largely set the agenda for subsequent discussion. The lengthy introduction to Fitzmyer's commentary on Luke (#19) marked the general acceptance of this new characterization of the Third Evangelist, who contributed more to the New Testament than any other writer (Luke-Acts—28%, Paul—23%). Scholars have continued to explore the relationship between Luke the Historian and Luke the Theologian as well as to delineate and integrate important Lukan themes.

99 J. C. O'Neill. *The Theology of Acts in Its Historical Setting.* London: SPCK, 1961.

> A study of Acts' milieu; perspective toward Jews, Judaism, and Jewish-Gentile relations; and christological titles. Concludes that, together with Luke's first volume, Acts is an apologetic written to the educated and influential at the center of Roman power.

100 H. Flender. *St. Luke: Theologian of Redemptive History.* London: SPCK, 1967.

Luke has solved the problem of "salvation as past event" by a vertical dimension, as distinct from Conzelmann's (#37) chronological dimension. Thus, a dialectical relationship exists between the presence of salvation in Christ's exaltation to heaven and its working out in the Christian community on earth.

101 W. G. Kümmel. "Current Theological Accusations against Luke." Translated from the German by W. C. Robinson Jr. *Andover Newton Quarterly* 16 (1975): 131–45. Original title: "Luc en accusation dans la théologie contemporaine." *Ephemerides Theologicae Lovanienses* 46 (1970): 265–81. German title: "Lukas in der Anklange der heutigen Theologie." *Zeitschrift für die neutestamentliche Wissenschaft* 63 (1972): 149–65. Reprinted as pp. 416–36 in *Das Lukas-Evangelium*. Edited by G. Braumann. Wege der Forschung 280. Darmstadt: Wissenschaftliche, 1974.

Discusses the major allegations against Lukan theology in the areas of eschatology, atonement, and early catholicism; yet argues for the basic soundness of Luke's theology of salvation-history and his agreement with the central tenets of New Testament faith.

102 J. Navone. *Themes of St. Luke*. Rome: Gregorian University, 1970.

A series of 20 thematic studies important to Luke—e.g., prayer, banquet, poor, and witness.

103 I. H. Marshall. *Luke: Historian and Theologian*. Contemporary Evangelical Perspectives. Grand Rapids: Zondervan, 1971. Second Edition: 1989.

An introduction to Luke's theology and, in effect, to Marshall's commentary on Luke (#18) emphasizing Luke's value as a historian, his theological accord with his sources, "salvation" as the key Lukan concept, and the need for critical assessment of current trends in Lukan studies. The second edition contains a final chapter (adapted from #10) surveying Lukan studies in the 1970s–'80s.

104 R. H. Smith. "The Theology of Acts." *Concordia Theological Monthly* 42 (1971): 527–35.

Emphasizes that Luke and Acts should be read as the unified work of a "brilliant theologian," that the conclusion in Rome is of ecclesiological import, and that Luke's focus on Paul's preaching of repentance intends to make the enthroned Jesus contemporary to each generation, overcoming the distance from his earthly ministry.

105 F. Neirynck (ed.). *L'Evangile de Luc: Problémes littéraires et théologiques. Mémorial Lucien Cerfaux.* BETL 32. Leuven: Leuven University Press, 1973. Revised and enlarged edition: L'Evangile de Luc—The Gospel of Luke, 1989.

Twelve textual and thematic studies in French from the 1968 Leuven colloquium on the Gospel of Luke, updated and supplemented in the revised edition by seven English contributions from twenty years later, including an outstanding essay assessing research on Luke 4:16–30 from 1972–89.

106 F. W. Danker. "Theological Presuppositions of St. Luke." *CTM* 4 (1977): 98–103.

Luke's theological presuppositions are in continuity with the Old Testament and the Apocrypha, as exemplified by the themes of God's power and human responsibility, God's impartiality, God's patience with sinners, inescapable judgment, resurrection, and paradise.

107 R. B. Sloan Jr. *The Favorable Year of the Lord: A Study of Jubilary Theology in the Gospel of Luke.* Austin, Tex.: Schola Press, 1977.

A study of the programmatic Jubilee text, Luke 4:16–30, and its thematic recurrence, underscoring its eschatological aspects and its relation to Luke's christology and purpose.

108 C. H. Talbert (ed.). *Perspectives on Luke-Acts.* Danville, Va.: Association of Baptist Professors of Religion/Edinburgh: T. & T. Clark, 1978.

A collection of introductory, exegetical, and thematic essays stemming from the Society of Biblical Literature Luke-Acts Group between 1972 and 1978.

109 D. J. Dupont. *The Salvation of the Gentiles: Essays on the Acts of the Apostles.* New York: Paulist, 1979.

A series of thematic studies on Acts covering the topics
of the Gentile mission and the theology of Acts, Pentecost, conversion, Christian communitarianism, and messianic and apologetic interpretation of the Old Testament.

110 D. Juel. *Luke-Acts: The Promise of History.* Atlanta: John
Knox, 1983.

An introduction to, and unified literary reading of, Luke's
two volumes. Addressed to Jewish Christians, Luke-Acts
is best understood from the perspective of "Jewish crisis
literature," seeking to discern God's hand in the tumul-
tuous times subsequent to the Jewish war.

111 R. F. O'Toole. *The Unity of Luke's Theology: An Analysis
of Luke-Acts.* Good News Studies 9. Wilmington, Del.:
Michael Glazier, 1984.

Employing composition criticism from a salvation-historical perspective, O'Toole seeks to demonstrate that
Luke subordinates all theological concerns to one dominant theme—that God continues to bring salvation to his
people, Israel, who are now the Christians. This salvation
is brought through Jesus' earthly life as well as his presence in his church.

112 C. H. Talbert (ed.). *Luke-Acts: New Perspectives from the
Society of Biblical Literature Seminar.* New York: Crossroad, 1984.

A collection of introductory, thematic, and exegetical
studies stemming directly or indirectly from the Society
of Biblical Literature Luke-Acts Seminar (1979–1983), intended to supplement *Perspectives on Luke-Acts* (#108).

113 R. J. Karris. *Luke: Artist and Theologian. Luke's Passion Account as Literature.* Theological Inquiries. New York/
Mawhah/Toronto: Paulist, 1985.

Examines Luke's major literary motifs and their recapit-
ulation in his passion account, seeking to explain through
Luke's literary artistry the reason for and significance of
Jesus' death.

114 R. F. O'Toole. "Highlights of Luke's Theology." *CTM* 12
(1985): 353–60.

Briefer development of #111, emphasizing such themes as universality, the disadvantaged, the delay of the parousia, peace with Rome, joy, and the imitation of Jesus.

115 J. A. Grassi. *God Makes Me Laugh: A New Approach to Luke.* Good News Studies 17. Wilmington, Del.: Michael Glazier, 1986.

Accessible, thematic study highlighting the comical, the paradoxical, and the unexpected as central components of the theology of Luke-Acts, emphasizing its continuity with and continuation of key Old Testament themes.

116 B. R. Gaventa. "Toward a Theology of Acts: Reading and Rereading." *Int* 42 (1988): 146–57.

Addresses the failure of the major methods of redaction criticism, analysis of speeches, consideration of key texts, and identification of theological themes to disclose fully the theology of Acts because they do not deal seriously with its character as *narrative.* "An adequate treatment of the theology of Acts needs to attend to the elements the narrative repeats, the information omitted, the appearance and disappearance of individuals and groups of people, the rich interweaving of story lines asking what each of those suggests about the theology of the author" (p. 157). Luke's theology of glory is considered as a test case.

117 J. A. Fitzmyer. *Luke the Theologian: Aspects of His Teaching.* New York/Mahwah: Paulist, 1989.

Eight studies on Lukan themes extending beyond or treating more comprehensively topics found in his commentary (#19), including authorship, the infancy narrative, Mary, John the Baptist, discipleship, Satan and demons, the Jewish people and the Law, and the death of Jesus.

118 N. H. Keathley (ed.). *With Steadfast Purpose: Essays on Acts in Honor of Henry Jackson Flanders Jr.* Waco, Tex.: Baylor University Press, 1990.

Fifteen essays employing diverse methodologies on themes and texts in Acts.

119 H. C. Kee. *Good News to the Ends of the Earth: The Theology of Acts.* Philadelphia: Trinity/London: SCM, 1990.

Concise theology of Acts incorporating insights from "the social, political, literary and cultural setting of the Roman world in which the early church was living and working" (p. 5); topics include Jesus as God's agent, the Spirit's role, religious and cultural boundaries, the functioning of the Christian community and the nature of Christian witness.

120 E. Richard (ed.). *New Views on Luke and Acts*. Collegeville, Minn.: Liturgical, 1990.

A collection of eleven essays stemming from the Catholic Biblical Association's Luke-Acts Task Force covering introductory, methodological, exegetical, theological, and thematic issues.

121 P. Luomanen (ed.). *Luke-Acts: Scandinavian Perspectives*. Publications of the Finnish Exegetical Society 54. Göttingen: Vandenhoeck & Ruprecht, 1991.

Collection of seven methodological, hermeneutical, and thematic essays representative of recent Scandinavian research on Luke-Acts.

122 G. O'Collins and G. Marconi (eds.). *Luke and Acts* (E. Rasco Festschrift). Translated by M. J. O'Connell. New York/Mahwah: Paulist, 1993. Original title: *Luca-Atti: Studi in onore di P. Emilio Rasco nel suo 70o compleanno*. Assisi: Cittadella, 1991.

A collection of thematic and exegetical essays on Luke-Acts examining such questions as Luke's view of the Old Testament, discipleship and mission, the Jews, Paul, and so on.

5.2 The Divine, the Demonic, and the Use of Israel's Scriptures

Composition and literary criticism of Luke-Acts have highlighted the import of God's purpose to the Third Evangelist. This is represented in a variety of ways in the narrative—e.g., by direct mention of the divine plan, with reference to the phrase "it is necessary" or "must," by appeals of diverse kinds to the Scriptures, by those who serve God's aim, and by the appearance of various forms of opposition to God's purpose in the narrative. More and

more, the pervasiveness of Luke's use of the Scriptures of Isracl
(whether explicit or by allusory echo) and the degree to which
Luke understands his two volumes as a self-conscious continuation of the story of the outworking of God's redemptive purpose
is recognized, as is the pervasive influence of Satan throughout
the narrative (*contra* #37).

123 J. W. Doeve. *Jewish Hermeneutics and the Synoptic Gospels
and Acts.* Assen, Netherlands: Van Gorcum, 1954.

> Attempts to locate scriptural interpretation in the Synop-
> tic Gospels and Acts within Jewish practices of using and
> expounding Scripture. Chapter 6 is devoted to scriptural
> exegesis in Acts 2:24–31; 13:24–38.

124 P. Schubert. "The Structure and Significance of Luke 24."
Pp. 165–86 in *Neutestamentliche Studien für Rudolf Bultmann zu seinem siebzigsten Geburtstag am 20. August
1954.* Edited by W. Eltester. Beihefte zur *Zeitschrift für die
neutestamentliche Wissenschaft* 21. Berlin: Alfred Töpel-
mann, 1954. Second edition: 1957.

> Luke's proof-from-prophecy theology is at center-stage in
> Luke 24.

125 D. J. Dupont. "Apologetic Use of the Old Testament in the
Acts of the Apostles." Translated by J. Keating. Pp. 129–59
in *The Salvation of the Gentiles: Essays on the Acts of the
Apostles.* New York: Paulist, 1979. Original title: "L'Utili-
sation Apologétique de L'Ancien Testament dans les dis-
cours des Actes." Pp. 245–82 in *Études sur les Actes des
Apôtres.* Paris: Du Cerf, 1967.

> An examination of quotations and allusions to the Old
> Testament in the speeches of Acts suggests that some
> passages evidence redaction of written source material;
> that the speeches in Acts presume the use of the Greek Bi-
> ble; that early Christian scriptural argumentation, for the
> most part, adheres closely to the meaning of the original;
> but that the Old Testament is in these addresses being
> read in the light of Christ, just as the significance of the
> Christ-event is shaped by the Old Testament.

126 D. J. Dupont. "Messianic Interpretation of the Psalms in the Acts of the Apostles." Translated by J. Keating. Pp. 103–28 in *The Salvation of the Gentiles: Essays on the Acts of the Apostles.* New York: Paulist, 1979. Original title: "L'Interprétation des Psaumes dans les Actes des Apôtres." Pp. 283–307 in *Études sur les Actes des Apôtres.* Paris: Du Cerf, 1967.

The characteristic reading of the Psalms in the early church took Christ as its primary point of reference.

127 J. A. Sanders. "From Isaiah 61 to Luke 4." Pp. 75–106 in *Christianity, Judaism and Other Greco-Roman Cults: Studies for Morton Smith at Sixty,* part one: *New Testament.* Edited by J. Neusner. Studies in Judaism in Late Antiquity 12. Leiden: Brill, 1975. Revised and reprinted in C. A. Evans and J. A. Sanders, *Luke and Scripture: Essays on the Authoritative Function of Sacred Tradition in Luke-Acts,* pp. 46–49. Minneapolis: Fortress, 1993.

Employing a method he calls "comparative midrash," Sanders argues that the citation of Isaiah 61:1–2/58:6 in Luke 4:18–19 builds on earlier interpretation of the Isaianic text, especially by countering partisan readings of God's blessing known to us from Qumran material.

128 G. D. Kilpatrick. "Some Quotations in Acts." Pp. 81–97 in *Les Actes des Apôtres: Traditions, Rédaction, Théologie.* Edited by J. Kremer. BETL 48. Leuven: Leuven University Press, 1979.

The citations of the Old Testament in Acts 1:20; 2:16–21; 3:22–23; 7:42–43, 49–50; 13:41; 15:16–18 derive from a pre-Christian Hellenistic Jewish collection; their appearance in Acts illustrates the continuity between the Hellenistic synagogue and the church.

129 D. Seccombe. "Luke and Isaiah." *NTS* 27 (1981): 252–59.

An examination of the Nazareth sermon (Luke 4:18–19) and the servant-theme in Luke-Acts suggests (1) the widespread import of Isaiah for Luke and (2) that, although Luke found Isaiah in his sources, the Evangelist worked with the Isaianic material within its context in Isaiah as a whole.

130 J. A. Sanders. "Isaiah in Luke." *Int* 36 (1982): 144–55. Revised and reprinted in C. A. Evans and J. A. Sanders, *Luke and Scripture: Essays on the Authoritative Function of Sacred Tradition in Luke-Acts*, pp. 14–25. Minneapolis: Fortress, 1993.

"Luke, steeped in the Old Testament, makes clear that to understand what God was doing in Christ, one has to know Scripture; and especially the Book of Isaiah" (p. 144).

131 A. T. Hanson. *The Living Utterances of God: The New Testament Exegesis of the Old*, pp. 78–89. London: Darton, Longman and Todd, 1983.

Luke's use of the Old Testament is second-hand through-and-through; only rarely did he turn directly to the Scriptures himself, preferring to draw on the exegesis available to him in his sources.

132 J. Jervell. "The Center of Scripture in Luke." Translated by R. A. Harrisville. Pp. 122–37 in *The Unknown Paul: Essays on Luke-Acts and Early Christian History*. Minneapolis: Augsburg, 1984. Original title: "Die Mitte der Schrift: Zum lukanischen Verständnis des Alten Testaments." Pp. 79–96 in *Die Mitte des Neuen Testaments: Einheit und Vielfalt neutestamentlicher Theologie. Festschrift für Eduard Schweizer zum siebzigsten Geburtstag*. Edited by U. Luz and H. Weder. Göttingen: Vandenhoeck & Ruprecht, 1983.

Argues that Luke sees the center of Scripture in its prophetic, and particularly messianic, aspect; this explains the importance of David and Moses in Luke-Acts, for these are both prophetic figures.

133 C. H. Cosgrove. "The Divine ΔΕΙ in Luke-Acts: Investigations into the Lukan Understanding of God's Providence." *NovT* 26 (1984): 168–90.

The "divine must" in Luke-Acts is rooted in God's ancient plan, constitutes a summons to obedience, is guaranteed by God, and dramatically highlights God's saving miracle.

134 C. H. Talbert. "Promise and Fulfillment in Lucan Theology." Pp. 91–103 in *Luke-Acts: New Perspectives from the*

Society of Biblical Literature. Edited by C. H. Talbert. New York: Crossroad, 1984.

Queries whether "proof from prophecy" (cf. #124) can be made to bear the influential role in Lukan theology given it by some interpreters; Luke's notion of "prophecy" was broader than his use of the Old Testament.

135 T. L. Brodie. "Towards Unravelling Luke's Use of the Old Testament: Luke 7.11–17 as an *Imitatio* of 1 Kings 17.17–24." *NTS* 32 (1986): 247–67.

Luke 7:11–17 shares a literary relationship with 1 Kings 17:17–24—a relationship best understood within the framework of Hellenistic "imitation"; because Hellenistic authors did not normally confine themselves to imitating isolated passages, this finding suggests more pervasive use of the LXX.

136 D. L. Bock. *Proclamation from Prophecy and Pattern: Lucan Old Testament Christology.* JSNTSS 12. Sheffield: JSOT Press, 1987.

Using a redaction-critical analysis, Bock surveys the use of the Old Testament from Luke 1 to Acts 13; he argues that Luke's interest is not so much in "proof from prophecy" (cf. #124) as in a proclamation of Jesus as universal Lord rooted in scriptural prophecies and patterns.

137 J. T. Sanders. "The Prophetic Use of the Scriptures in Luke-Acts." Pp. 191–98 in *Early Jewish and Christian Exegesis: Studies in Memory of William Hugh Brownlee.* Edited by C. A. Evans and W. G. Stinespring. Atlanta: Scholars Press, 1987.

For Luke, the Scriptures function primarily as something to be fulfilled, as prophetic; they prophesy Jesus' death and resurrection and the beginning of Christianity as well as the rejection of the gospel by the Jews and its acceptance by the Gentiles.

138 J. B. Tyson. "The Gentile Mission and the Authority of Scripture in Acts." *NTS* 33 (1987): 619–31.

Argues that Luke's view of Scripture is utilitarian—that it is authoritative when it is useful and correctly interpreted, but can at times be amended by God, Jesus, or the Spirit.

139 R. W. Wall. "Peter, 'Son' of Jonah: The Conversion of Cornelius in the Context of the Canon." *JSNT* 29 (1987): 79–90. Reprinted in R. W. Wall and E. E. Lemcio, *The New Testament as Canon: A Reader in Canonical Criticism*, pp. 129–40. JSNTSS 76. Sheffield: JSOT Press, 1992.

Luke's narrative of Acts 10:1–11:18 draws on important echoes of the story of Jonah—thus identifying Jonah's God as Peter's God and calling into question sectarianism within the church.

140 C. K. Barrett. "Luke/Acts." Pp. 213–44 in *It Is Written: Scripture Citing Scripture. Essays in Honour of Barnabas Lindars, S. S. F.* Edited by D. A. Carson and H. G. M. Williamson. Cambridge: Cambridge University Press, 1988.

A survey of scriptural citations—in Luke's Gospel in comparison with Mark and Matthew, and in Acts under the themes: preaching, prayer, and direction for the church's life.

141 J. A. Fitzmyer. "Satan and Demons in Luke-Acts." Pp. 146–74 in *Luke the Theologian: Aspects of His Teaching.* New York/Mahwah: Paulist, 1989.

A study of the Lukan terminology of Satan and the demonic, the temptation narrative of Luke 4, Conzelmann's (#37) alleged Satan-free period of Jesus' ministry, and the enigmatic saying of Jesus in Luke 10:17–20 leads Fitzmyer to conclude that the primary function of Satan in Luke is to highlight Jesus' role in proclaiming the kingdom.

142 S. R. Garrett. *The Demise of the Devil: Magic and the Demonic in Luke's Writings.* Minneapolis: Fortress, 1989.

Employing socio-historical and literary methods, Garrett explores (1) the role of Satan behind manifestations of magic in Luke-Acts and as the prime adversary working against God's purpose; and (2) how Luke highlights for his audience that Christ had conquered Satan and his agents, whether human or supernatural.

143 B. J. Koet. *Five Studies on Interpretation of Scripture in Luke-Acts.* Studiorum Novi Testamenti Auxilia 14. Leuven: Leuven University Press, 1989.

An examination of the significance of Scripture for Luke via an exploration of Luke 4:16–30; 24:13–35; Acts 23:42–52; 28:16–31; and Paul as an interpreter of Scripture in Acts.

144 W. H. Bellinger Jr. "The Psalms and Acts: Reading and Rereading." Pp. 127–43 in *With Steadfast Purpose: Essays on Acts in Honor of Henry Jackson Flanders Jr.* Edited by N. H. Keathley. Waco, Tex.: Baylor University Press, 1990.

An exploration of an intertextual reading of Psalms 2 and 16 in Acts—moving from the Old Testament texts to their use in Acts, and from their use in Acts back to the Psalms.

145 L. M. Maloney. *"All That God Had Done with Them": The Narration of the Works of God in the Early Christian Community as Described in the Acts of the Apostles.* American University Studies 7, Theology and Religion 91. New York/Bern/Frankfurt/Paris: Peter Lang, 1991.

Argues from an examination of Luke 24:33–35; Acts 4:23–31; 11:1–18; 12:1–17; 14:26–28; 15:1–35; and 21:15–20 that Luke made use of a schematic pattern of reporting on God's activity (i.e., transition, arrival, assembly, report, response) in order to underscore the certainty that God's work was ongoing in the community of believers.

146 J. T. Squires. *The Plan of God in Luke-Acts.* SNTSMS 76. Cambridge: Cambridge University Press, 1993.

Traces the development of the theme "plan of God" throughout Luke-Acts by attending to direct statements by the author and to other narrative indications—e.g., signs and wonders, divine appearances, fulfillment of prophecy, and so on. Locates Luke-Acts on the map of Hellenistic historiography, with its emphasis in the programmatic role of providence.

147 J. B. Green. "The Problem of a Beginning: Israel's Scriptures in Luke 1–2." *Bulletin of Biblical Research* 4 (1994).

A narratological study of Luke 1–2, focusing above all on an examination of the plethora of echoes of the Abrahamic story of Genesis, leads to the conclusion that the "beginning" of Luke-Acts can be located only in God's purpose as articulated in the Scriptures of Israel; at this point at least, the framework with which Luke is working is not "promise-fulfillment," but rather a self-conscious continuation of the redemptive story.

5.3 The Holy Spirit

From the opening of Luke's Gospel through Pentecost and the consequent account of the church's mission, the Holy Spirit plays a central role in the Lukan narrative. Contemporary study has focused on three questions. First, what is the relation in Luke-Acts between conversion and the coming of the Spirit—especially in light of 20th-century Pentecostal thought and the apparent irregularities of experience in Acts 8:4–25; 19:1–7? Second, what is the connection between Jesus' endowment with the Spirit (Luke 3:21–22; 4:18–19; Acts 10:37–38) and the outpouring of the Spirit at Pentecost and subsequently (e.g., Acts 2:1–4; 10:47; 11:16–17)? This issue is related to the larger question of the Lukan conception of the unity or segmentation of salvation history—with some emphasizing the continuity between the Spirit's work in the Old Testament, in Jesus' ministry, and in the church's mission, while others see a qualitative distinction between these. Finally, the purpose of the Spirit's presence in Luke-Acts is disputed.

148 G. W. H. Lampe. "The Holy Spirit in the Writings of St. Luke." Pp. 159–200 in *Studies in the Gospels: Essays in Memory of R. H. Lightfoot.* Edited by D. E. Nineham. Oxford: Blackwell, 1955.

A lengthy survey of the operation of God's Spirit in Luke-Acts, the activity of which unites Luke-Acts with the Old Testament, and the activity of Jesus with that of his followers.

149 J. H. E. Hull. *The Holy Spirit in the Acts of the Apostles.* London: Lutterworth, 1967.

For Luke, the church received the Spirit especially in order to engage in the evangelization of the world.

150 J. D. G. Dunn. *Baptism in the Holy Spirit: A Re-examination of the New Testament Teaching on the Gift of the Spirit in Relation to Pentecostalism Today,* pp. 38–102. Studies in Biblical Theology. London: SCM/Philadelphia: Westminster, 1970.

In dialogue especially with Pentecostals, Dunn insists that the gift of the Spirit is the only thing that makes one a Christian, the central element of Christian conversion-initiation.

151 F. F. Bruce. "The Holy Spirit in the Acts of the Apostles." *Int* 27 (1973): 166–83.

A survey oriented especially around the notion that Acts is concerned with "the age of the Spirit," with the spread of the gospel proceeding under the direction of the Holy Spirit.

152 J. D. G. Dunn. *Jesus and the Spirit: A Study of the Religious and Charismatic Experience of Jesus and the First Christians as Reflected in the New Testament,* pp. 136–96. London: SCM/Philadelphia: Westminster, 1975.

The charismatic experience of the earliest Christian communities as portrayed in Acts—including its sense of fellowship and mission and its ecstatic experiences—was grounded in Jesus' experience and continuing authority.

153 S. Brown. "'Water Baptism' and 'Spirit-Baptism' in Luke-Acts." *Anglican Theological Review* 59 (1977): 135–51.

Argues that Jesus' promise of the gift of the Spirit was not to individual believers, but rather was fulfilled once and for all at Pentecost; subsequent generations of Christians are to continue in the faith of the Spirit-filled apostles.

154 C. K. Barrett. "Light on the Holy Spirit from Simon Magnus (Acts 8,4–25)." Pp. 281–95 in *Les Actes des Apôtres: Traditions, Rédaction, Théologie.* Edited by J. Kremer. BETL 48. Leuven: Leuven University Press, 1979.

The church, for Luke, is the institutional home of the Spirit, but the church never controls or possesses the Spirit.

155 V. C. Pfitzner. "'Pneumatic' Apostleship? Apostle and Spirit in the Acts of the Apostles." Pp. 210–35 in *Wort in der Zeit: Neutestamentliche Studien. Festgabe für Karl Heinrich Rengstorf zum 75. Geburtstag.* Edited by W. Haubeck and M. Bachmann. Leiden: Brill, 1980.

> The repeated connection between the apostolate and the Spirit in Acts serves Luke's notion of salvation-historical continuity between divine activity in the Old Testament, in the ministry of Jesus, among the Twelve, and in the mission to the Gentiles; Luke's presentation of the Spirit thus legitimates the universality of the Gospel.

156 M. M. B. Turner. "Jesus and the Spirit in Lucan Perspective." *TynB* 32 (1981): 3–42.

> Against Dunn (#152) et al., Jesus' relationship to the Spirit is not archetypal for his disciples in Luke-Acts; rather, Jesus' ascension marks a new sphere of activity of the Spirit, wherein Jesus has lordship over the gift of the Spirit to the church.

157 M. M. B. Turner. "The Significance of Receiving the Spirit in Luke-Acts: A Survey of Modern Scholarship." *Trinity Journal* 2 (1981): 131–58.

> A critical survey of late 19th- and 20th-century attempts to interpret Luke's phrase, "to receive the Holy Spirit."

158 M. M. B. Turner. "Spirit Endowment in Luke-Acts: Some Linguistic Considerations." *Vox Evangelica* 12 (1981): 45–63.

> Attempts to clarify what *type* of language is being used when the Lukan narrative speaks of Spirit endowment (e.g., literal or non-literal) and to define what Luke's terminology intends to say about the Spirit's work.

159 H. M. Ervin. *Conversion-Initiation and the Baptism of the Holy Spirit.* Peabody, Mass.: Hendrickson, 1984.

> A point-by-point critique of #150, arguing against Dunn's notion that "repentance, faith, baptism, *and* the gift of the Holy Spirit represent an indivisible unity without which one is not a Christian" (vii) in favor of the classical Pentecostal view that the baptism in the Spirit is subsequent to new birth.

160 J. Jervell. "Sons of the Prophets: The Holy Spirit in the Acts of the Apostles." Pp. 96–121 in *The Unknown Paul: Essays on Luke-Acts and Early Christian History*. Minneapolis: Augsburg, 1984.

In Acts the Spirit confirms and supports the prophecy of the Scriptures regarding the identity of the church and the inclusion of Gentiles as God's people

161 R. Stronstad. *The Charismatic Theology of St. Luke*. Peabody, Mass.: Hendrickson, 1984.

Arguing for the literary and theological unity of Luke-Acts, the theological nature of Luke's historiography, and the independence of Luke (from Paul) as a theologian, Stronstad contends that for Luke the activity of the Spirit is not related particularly to conversion or to sanctification but to service in redemptive mission.

162 W. Russell. "The Anointing with the Holy Spirit in Luke-Acts." *Trinity Journal* 7 (1986): 47–63.

Argues for the continuity of the Holy Spirit's ministry in Jesus' life and in the life of the church by means of the experience of the anointing with the Spirit.

163 R. P. Menzies. *The Development of Early Christian Pneumatology: With Special Reference to Luke-Acts*. JSNTSS 54. Sheffield: JSOT Press, 1991.

Based on his extensive survey of the literature of "intertestamental Judaism" and a redactional analysis of Luke-Acts, Menzies argues that Luke, influenced by the dominant Jewish perception, consistently portrays the gift of the Spirit as a prophetic endowment for special insight and inspired speech.

164 J. B. Shelton. *Mighty in Word and Deed: The Role of the Holy Spirit in Luke-Acts*. Peabody, Mass.: Hendrickson, 1991.

A redaction-critical analysis, indicating that Luke's predominant interest in the Holy Spirit is empowerment for witness.

165 M. M. B. Turner. "The Spirit and the Power of Jesus' Miracles in the Lucan Conception." *NovT* 33 (1991): 124–52.

Luke associates the activity of the Spirit with prophecy, preaching, *and* miracles (e.g., healing and exorcism; *contra*, e.g., Menzies [#163]).

166 M. M. B. Turner. "The Spirit of Prophecy and the Power of Authoritative Preaching in Luke-Acts: A Question of Origins." *NTS* 38 (1992): 66–88.

Luke's understanding of the Spirit, especially as the power of charismatic preaching, owes more to his contacts with widespread Christian ideas than to an alleged Jewish view of the Spirit as "the Spirit of prophecy" (*contra*, e.g., Menzies [#163]).

5.4 Jesus of Nazareth: Lord and Christ

With the recognition of Luke the theologian came the question of the christology of Luke-Acts. P. Vielhaeur (#468) concluded that Lukan christology is pre-Pauline, while other scholars sought to determine whether Acts retains primitive christological traditions of the early church or exhibits that of Luke's day. Jesus' ascension and departure from the narrative in Acts has fostered discussion concerning the meaning of his exaltation and questions concerning a "christology of absence," Christ's relation to the Spirit, and the functioning of the church in his "name." Discussion of the christological titles in Luke-Acts have continued as a topic of lively debate. (On the controversy surrounding the soteriological significance of Jesus' death in Luke-Acts, see §5.6.)

167 J. A. T. Robinson. "The Most Primitive Christology of All?" *JTS* n.s. 7 (1956): 177–89.

Asserts that two primitive and conflicting christologies may be detected in Acts 2 and 3.

168 J. E. Ménard. "*Pais Theou* as Messianic Title in the Book of Acts." *CBQ* 19 (1957): 83–92.

Asks whether the title *pais theou* ("Servant of God") in Acts is limited to the early Jerusalem community since it does not occur in the Synoptics; concludes that this christology reflects a theological development of the church which, though early, is not primitive.

169 S. S. Smalley. "The Christology of Acts." *ExpTim* 73 (1962): 358–62.

Focuses on the speeches in Acts, their historicity, and their alleged levels of christology; concludes that Luke was acquainted with and used the "basic materials" of christology current in the Jewish-Christian world to articulate a non-adoptionistic, catholic, high christology.

170 C. F. D. Moule. "The Christology of Acts." Pp. 159–85 in *Studies in Luke-Acts* (P. Schubert Festschrift). Edited by L. E. Keck and J. L. Martyn. Nashville: Abingdon, 1966.

Compares the christology of Acts with the Gospel of Luke and other New Testament writings, concluding that the variety of christologies in Acts is linked to and gives evidence of Luke's use of sources.

171 D. L. Jones. "The Title *Christos* in Luke-Acts." *CBQ* 32 (1970): 69–76.

Redactional study of the use of the term *Christos* ("Christ") in Luke and analysis of its occurrences in the speeches in Acts, concluding that Luke's usage reveals more concerning the christology of Luke's day than that of the earliest Christian community.

172 I. H. Marshall. "The Resurrection in the Acts of the Apostles." Pp. 92–107 in *Apostolic History and the Gospel: Biblical and Historical Essays Presented to F. F. Bruce on His 60th Birthday*. Edited by W. W. Gasque and R. P. Martin. Grand Rapids: Eerdmans/Exeter: Paternoster, 1970.

The central position Acts gives to Jesus' resurrection "as the decisive act whereby in accordance with prophecy God exalted his Son to be the Lord and revealed him to chosen witnesses in order that they might preach the good news of forgiveness in his name" (p. 107) is firmly based on tradition.

173 G. W. MacRae. "'Whom Heaven Must Receive Until the Time': Reflections on the Christology of Acts." *Int* 27 (1973): 151–65.

Considers facets of the Lukan christological dialectic of "absence/presence." Though absent since his ascension, Christ is present in various ways, as evidenced by his titles, the presence of the Holy Spirit, his name, his presence as a "part of history," and his model of discipleship fulfilled in his followers.

174 I. H. Marshall. "The Resurrection of Jesus in Luke." *TynB* 24 (1973): 55–98.

Judicious, scene-by-scene study of the resurrection of Jesus in Luke, from burial to ascension, employing theological, stylistic, and tradition-historical criteria to uncover the historical basis of the account. While contending for a historic core, this study concludes with a discussion of symbolic elements in the Lukan record.

175 S. S. Smalley. "The Christology of Acts Again." Pp. 79–93 in *Christ and the Spirit in the New Testament: Studies in Honour of Charles Francis Digby Moule*. Edited by B. Lindars and S. S. Smalley. Cambridge: Cambridge University Press, 1973.

An examination of the christology of 1 Peter and of the Petrine material in Acts points to the essentially primitive character of the latter.

176 E. Franklin. *Christ the Lord: A Study in the Purpose and Theology of Luke-Acts*. Philadelphia: Westminster/London: SPCK, 1975.

Employing redaction criticism and running counter to such "received opinions" as H. Conzelmann (#37), P. Vielhauer (#468), and E. Haenchen (#29), Franklin understands Luke as a pastoral theologian seeking to renew eschatological expectation; salvation history does not replace imminent eschatology but reinforces it. Old Testament promises have been fulfilled in Jesus, the restoration of Israel, and the incorporation of the Gentiles, which is the final fulfillment. The topics of subordinate christology, Luke's alleged Paulinisms, and Luke's ethics are also engaged.

177 R. F. O'Toole. "Luke's Understanding of Jesus' Resurrection-Ascension-Exaltation." *BTB* 9 (1979): 106–14.

Review of the major scholarly interpretations of this theme, emphasizing the need for a more holistic methodology which looks at the totality of Luke-Acts. Jesus' resurrection in Luke is multifaceted, incorporating aspects of Davidic messianism but also drawing a connection between Son, kingdom, and Son of Man.

178 J. A. Ziesler. "The Name of Jesus in the Acts of the Apostles." *JSNT* 4 (1979): 28–41.

Refutes the theory that Luke uses the concept of "the name of Jesus" to convey the presence of an otherwise absent Lord. Rather, it is used to connect Jesus' name with the gospel in the contexts of baptism, preaching, teaching, and healing.

179 D. L. Tiede. *Prophecy and History in Luke-Acts*. Philadelphia: Fortress, 1980.

Luke writes to primarily Jewish Christians to explain suffering after the Jewish war. As did Christ, Christians suffer because of their faithfulness, but also take part in the sufferings of Israel, which have come because of the rejection of Messiah. However, this "time of the Gentiles" is not final rejection, but will be followed by the restoration of Israel.

180 R. F. O'Toole. "Activity of the Risen Jesus in Luke-Acts." *Biblica* 4 (1981): 471–98.

Emphasizes the activity of the risen Jesus, contrary to other scholarly opinions, underscoring his presence in the Eucharist, the Spirit, preaching, his name, salvation, and in signs and wonders.

181 D. L. Jones. "The Title 'Servant' in Luke-Acts." Pp. 148–65 in *Luke-Acts: New Perspectives from the Society of Biblical Literature Seminar*. Edited by C. H. Talbert. New York: Crossroad, 1984.

Concludes, *contra* Harnack, Jeremias, and Cullmann, that a primitive servant christology did not exist in the earliest Christian community. Luke-Acts reflects the developed christology of Luke and the Christian community at the end of the first century.

182 D. L. Jones. "The Title *Huios Theou* in Acts." Pp. 451–63 in *Society of Biblical Literature 1985 Seminar Papers*. Edited by K. H. Richards. Atlanta: Scholars Press, 1985.

Examines Luke's use of this christological title (i.e., "Son of God") as influenced by the Hellenistic *theios anēr* ("divine man") concept; as synonymous with the title "Christ"; as applied by God, Satan, angels, and demons in the Gospel; and as used by Paul in reference to Jesus' resurrection-exaltation.

183 M. M. B. Turner. "The Spirit of Christ and Christology." Pp. 168–90 in *Christ the Lord: Studies in Christology Presented to Donald Guthrie*. Edited by H. H. Rowdon. Downers Grove, Ill.: InterVarsity/Leicester: Inter-Varsity Press, 1985.

Studies Jesus' relation to the Spirit in Peter's Pentecost speech for its christological implications. Concludes that "the church was confronted with a Jesus who was Lord of the Spirit: the Spirit of God had become the Spirit of Jesus too, and that would most probably have been understood as a revelation of Jesus' divine nature, and fitting grounds for worshipping him" (p. 190).

184 J. M. Dawsey. "The Unexpected Christ: The Lucan Image." *ExpTim* 98 (1987): 296–300.

Exploration of how the Lukan Jesus is portrayed in both preconceived notions—exemplified by Elijah, Moses, and David typology; as well as paradoxical—as seen by his presence/absence in the Emmaus episode.

185 J. A. Fitzmyer. "Jesus in the Early Church through the Eyes of Luke-Acts." *Scripture Bulletin* 17 (1987): 26–35.

The Lukan portrayal of Jesus is developed in relation to Luke's kerygma; the geographical and historical horizons; christological titles; and Jesus and the Spirit; underscoring Luke's preservation of, and unique contribution to, primitive christology.

186 D. Senior. *The Passion of Jesus in the Gospel of Luke*. Passion Series 3. Wilmington, Del.: Michael Glazier, 1989.

Redaction-critical study of Luke's passion account, preceded by a synopsis of Lukan themes leading up to the death of Jesus, and concluding with a synthesis of the meaning of the passion relevant to Luke's understanding of evil, the Christian community, and soteriology.

187 D. D. Sylva (ed.). *Reimaging the Death of the Lukan Jesus.*
AMTBBB 73. Frankfurt: Anton Hain, 1990.

Eight essays focusing on the specifically Lukan understanding of Jesus' suffering and death. Attention is given
to Luke's presentation of the crucifixion; Old Testament,
Intertestamental, and Greco-Roman backgrounds; development of characters; and the "spatial setting" of Jesus'
death.

188 D. Crump. *Jesus the Intercessor.* WUNT 2:49. Tübingen:
Mohr, 1992.

In Luke-Acts we find a "narrative explanation" of previous Christian confessions concerning Jesus as the unique,
heavenly intercessor. Jesus' prayer ministry demonstrates that he is the exalted, human intercessor par ex-
cellence *vis-à-vis* Judaism, that he is the pastoral model
for Christians, and how Jesus mediates salvation through
his prayers.

5.5 Judaism, the Jewish People, and the Gentiles

The question of Luke's relationship to Judaism is one of the
most hotly contested in modern Lukan studies. Viewpoints range
widely, with some insisting that Luke is irretrievably anti-Jewish
(some believe that Luke thinks the time of Israel is past without
indicting him so strongly), while others (admittedly a minority)
hold that Luke-Acts originates from within a vital Jewish-Christian church. This diversity arises in large part from the complexity of the Lukan portrayal of Jewish institutions (esp. the temple)
and groups (esp. the Pharisees). All agree that the inclusion of the
Gentiles is a crucial concern for Luke, but this issue has raised
further questions related to the nature of the Gentiles and the
presence of "God-fearers" in Luke's narrative.

189 D. J. Dupont. "The Salvation of the Gentiles and the Theological Significance of Acts." Translated by J. Keating. Pp.
11–33 in *The Salvation of the Gentiles: Essays on the Acts
of the Apostles.* New York: Paulist, 1979. Original title: "Le
Salut des Gentils et la Signification Théologique du Livre

des Actes." Pp. 393–419 in *Études sur les Actes des Apôtres*. Paris: Du Cerf, 1967.

Luke's purpose in writing Acts was to indicate how the message of salvation reached "the end of the earth"—that is, "how the apostolic preaching turned toward the pagan world" (p. 33).

190 J. Jervell. *Luke and the People of God: A New Look at Luke-Acts*. Minneapolis: Augsburg, 1972.

A collection of essays concerned above all with the problem of the identity of the church as Israel—including obedient Jews who believe in Jesus and believing Gentiles. Classic statement of the position that the Gentile mission in Luke-Acts derives not from Jewish rejection of the gospel but from its acceptance by some Jews.

191 C. Van der Waal. "The Temple in the Gospel According to Luke." *Neotestamentica* 7 (1973) 44–59.

The apostasy of Israel in rejecting its Messiah resulted in the destruction of Jerusalem and the temple.

192 S. G. Wilson. *The Gentiles and the Gentile Mission in Luke-Acts*. SNTSMS 23. Cambridge: Cambridge University Press, 1973.

Contends that Luke lacks any developed, consistent theology of the Gentiles, but rather, as a pastor and historian, drew together a number of disparate themes to show how the development of Gentile churches had its origin in Judaism and was rooted in the Old Testament.

193 J. A. Ziesler. "Luke and the Pharisees." *NTS* 25 (1979): 146–57.

Unlike the other Evangelists, Luke is able to present the Pharisees in a favorable light, at least in part; this suggests a Lukan community where the Pharisees were not regarded uniformly as enemies and that church-Pharisee relations differed from place to place.

194 J. M. Dawsey. "The Origin of Luke's Positive Perception of the Temple." *PRS* 18 (1981): 5–22.

In presenting the Jerusalem temple in a positive light, Luke is representing early Christian tradition that pre-

dates Mark—in fact, which may actually reach back to
the earliest Christian community in Jerusalem.

195 A. T. Kraabel. "The Disappearance of the 'God-fearers.'"
Numen 28 (1981): 113–26.

Recent studies call into question archaeological and epigraphic evidence once offered for God-fearers, suggesting
that their appearance in Acts is motivated by theological
and narrative purposes.

196 F. D. Weinert. "The Meaning of the Temple in Luke-Acts."
BTB 11 (1981): 85–89.

"In his Gospel and in Acts Luke highlights the Temple as
that ancient and renowned site in Israel which is specifically suited to promoting the service of God through
pious observance, prayer, praise, and public testimony"
(p. 89).

197 M. Wilcox. "The 'God-fearers' in Acts: A Reconsideration."
JSNT 13 (1981): 102–22.

Questions the widespread view that the phrases "those
who fear God" and "those who revere God" refer to a
class of Gentiles drawn to Judaism without actually becoming Jews; suggests only "the pious" are in view,
whether they be Jew or Gentile, proselyte or "adherent."

198 S. G. Wilson. *Luke and the Law*. SNTSMS 50. Cambridge:
Cambridge University Press, 1983.

Luke's intended audience was primarily Gentile—for
whom the law was non-binding; the law could nevertheless be presented positively since for Jewish Christians
even zealous observance could be a legitimate expression
of piety.

199 C. L. Blomberg. "The Law in Luke-Acts." *JSNT* 22 (1984):
53–80.

Luke portrays Christianity as free from the law as "a reg-
ulatory code of behavior," and concerned with law only
as it was fulfilled in and interpreted by Jesus.

200 J. L. Houlden. "The Purpose of Luke." *JSNT* 21 (1984): 53–
65.

Maddox (#88) has not taken seriously enough the complexity of Luke's portrait of Judaism in his overly negative assessment of that portrait; to the contrary, Luke wanted to demonstrate how Christian beginnings were rooted in Jewish piety. On the one hand, Christians should not easily dismiss Judaism, while on the other, Jews were invited to accept God's purpose as fulfilled in Christ.

201 T. M. Finn. "The God-Fearers Reconsidered." *CBQ* 47 (1985): 75–84.

A re-examination of the extant evidence indicates that "God-fearers" became a technical designation only in the second century, that Luke's straight-line trajectory, Jews—God-fearers—Gentiles, oversimplified the spread of early Christianity.

202 R. C. Tannehill. "Israel in Luke-Acts: A Tragic Story." *JBL* 104 (1985): 69–85.

Luke guides his readers to experience the story of Israel and its Messiah as a tragic story—raising expectations for Israel's salvation through Jesus in Luke 1–2 that go unfulfilled in the narrative as a whole.

203 *Biblical Archaeology Review* 12 (1986): 44–63.

A continuation of the conversation begun in #195. R. S. MacLennan and T. A. Kraabel summarize and add to the material in #195 in "The God-fearers: A Literary and Theological Invention" (46–53). R. E. Tannenbaum discusses archaeological data related to "Jews and God-fearers in the Holy City of Aphrodite" (54–57). L. H. Feldman argues from evidence outside of Acts that there was a substantial group of Gentiles who were sympathetic to Judaism, for whom early Christianity might have had special appeal, in "The Omnipresence of the God-fearers" (58–63).

204 J. G. Gager. "Jews, Gentiles, and Synagogues in the Book of Acts." *Harvard Theological Review* 79 (1986): 91–99.

In conversation with Kraabel (#195), Gager argues that Luke's contribution to the meaning of "God-fearers" was

his view that they abandoned Judaism for Christianity—
a view for which there is no support outside Acts.

205 L. Gaston. "Anti-Judaism and the Passion Narrative in Luke
and Acts." Pp. 127–53 in *Anti-Judaism in Early Christianity*, Vol. 1: *Paul and the Gospels*. Edited by P. Richardson
and D. Granskou. Studies in Christianity and Judaism 2.
Waterloo: Wilfred Laurier University Press, 1986.

   The anti-Judaism of the Lukan passion narrative is extreme and stands in tension with the more pro-Jewish
material in Luke's Gospel and elsewhere in Acts.

206 J. B. Tyson. *The Death of Jesus in Luke-Acts*. Columbia,
S.C.: University of South Carolina Press, 1986.

   A literary analysis of the death of Jesus in Luke-Acts, focusing on the theme of conflict between Jesus and Jewish
people and institutions; argues that Luke's community
was associated with Gentiles rather than Jews.

207 R. L. Brawley. *Luke-Acts and the Jews: Conflict, Apology,
and Conciliation*. Society of Biblical Literature Monograph
Series 33. Atlanta: Scholars Press, 1987.

   Against those who read Luke-Acts as the triumph of Gentile Christianity over Judaism, Brawley finds in Lukan
thought an attitude of conciliation: Luke "draws what he
considers to be authentic Jews toward Christians and authentic Christians toward Judaism" (p. 159).

208 J. T. Sanders. *The Jews in Luke-Acts*. Philadelphia: Fortress,
1987.

   According to the narrative of Luke-Acts, Luke is irre-
pressibly hostile toward the Jewish people, who are themselves hostile toward the purposes of God.

209 J. T. Carroll. "Luke's Portrayal of the Pharisees." *CBQ* 50
(1988): 604–21.

   Luke portrays the Pharisees as an important link rooting
the Gentile Christian movement in its Jewish heritage;
the absence of the Pharisees from the major trial scenes of
Luke-Acts serves this legitimating function.

210 J. B. Chance. *Jerusalem, the Temple, and the New Age in
Luke-Acts*. Macon, Ga.: Mercer University Press, 1988.

A discussion of Luke's understanding of the significance of Jerusalem and the temple within the context of the Lukan eschatology.

211 F. G. Downing. "Law and Custom: Luke-Acts and Late Hellenism." Pp. 148–58, 187–91 in *Law and Religion: Essays on the Place of the Law in Israel and Early Christianity by Members of the Ehrhardt Seminar*. Edited by B. Lindars. Cambridge: James Clarke, 1988.

Luke presents the early Christian movement to the wider Hellenistic world as appropriately pious, but without restrictions that would be regarded as superstitious or overly rigid.

212 J. A. Overman. "The God-Fearers: Some Neglected Features." *JSNT* 32 (1988): 17–26.

Contra Kraabel (#195), there are historical reasons to believe that Luke's *picture* (if not *vocabulary*) of sympathetic Gentiles associated with the synagogue is a reflection of reality in the first-century diaspora.

213 J. B. Tyson (ed.). *Luke-Acts and the Jewish People: Eight Critical Perspectives*. Minneapolis: Augsburg, 1988.

An excellent point-of-entry into current discussion on this central issue in contemporary study of Luke-Acts, with contributions from J. Jervell, D. L. Tiede, D. P. Moessner, J. T. Sanders, M. Salmon, R. C. Tannehill, M. J. Cook, and J. B. Tyson.

214 J. A. Fitzmyer. "The Jewish People and the Mosaic Law in Luke-Acts." Pp. 175–202 in *Luke the Theologian: Aspects of His Teaching*. New York/Mahwah: Paulist, 1989.

Luke writes for a predominately Gentile church to explain how "the law and the prophets" themselves provided for Gentile inclusion in the divine promises made to Israel.

215 C. H. Gempf. "The God-Fearers." Pp. 444–47 in C. J. Hemer, *The Book of Acts in the Setting of Hellenistic History*. Edited by C. H. Gempf. WUNT 49. Tübingen: Mohr, 1989.

Contra Kraabel (#195), "God-fearers" could be used to designate a significant number of Gentiles sympathetic to though not full members of the Jewish community, who would have been ripe for conversion to Christianity; the evidence is insufficient, however, to prove the complete accuracy of Acts in its use of similar terminology.

216 D. P. Moessner. "Paul in Acts: Preacher of Eschatological Repentance to Israel." *NTS* 34 (1989): 96–104.

A comparison of Jesus' pronouncements of eschatological judgment in Luke with those of Paul in Acts, underscoring the unity of believing and unbelieving Jews as God's people Israel, the continuing opportunity for Jewish repentance, and the emphatic warning to Israel at the end of Acts.

217 J. A. Weatherly. "The Jews in Luke-Acts." *TynB* 40 (1989): 107–17.

A critical assessment of the work of Sanders (#208), arguing that an accurate assessment of the Jews in Luke-Acts must balance both positive and negative elements in their portrayal. The widespread rejection of Jesus and the gospel by Jews according to Luke is christologically motivated, vindicating Jesus as a true prophet.

218 C. A. Evans. "Is Luke's View of the Jewish Rejection of Jesus Anti-Semitic?" Pp. 29–56, 174–83 in *Reimaging the Death of the Lukan Jesus.* Edited by D. D. Sylva. AMTBBB 73. Frankfurt: Anton Hain, 1990.

Luke emphasizes Jewish responsibility for Jesus' crucifixion in order to locate the cross within the framework of the history of Israel, not as a consequence of any anti-Jewish sentiment.

219 I. A. Levinskaya. "The Inscription from Aphrodisias and the Problem of God-Fearers." *TynB* 41 (1990): 312–18.

Argues that this inscription provides clear evidence for the use of "God-fearer" to describe a Gentile sympathizer with Judaism, and lends support to the presence of this group in the world described in Acts.

220 F. J. Matera. "Responsibility for the Death of Jesus According to the Acts of the Apostles." *JSNT* 39 (1990): 77–93.

Although the speeches in Acts accuse the Jerusalemites of crucifying Jesus, these accusations are not anti-Jewish *per se* and Luke is not essentially hostile toward the Jewish people; rather, they function to call people to repentance.

221 D. P. Moessner. "The 'Leaven of the Pharisees' and 'This Generation': Israel's Rejection of Jesus according to Luke." Pp. 79–107, 190–93 in *Reimaging the Death of the Lukan Jesus*. Edited by D. D. Sylva. AMTBBB 73. Frankfurt: Anton Hain, 1990.

An exploration of the apparent tension between Luke's presentation of the leaders of Israel as the primary forces behind Jesus' crucifixion and the absence of any Pharisees from the number of those leaders, in spite of the leadership of the Pharisees in the opposition toward Jesus throughout most of the Gospel.

222 M. A. Powell. "The Religious Leaders in Luke: A Literary-Critical Study." *JBL* 109 (1990): 93–110.

A narrative-critical analysis of the religious leaders in Luke as characters within the narrative: (1) who serve as negative examples of discipleship, (2) whose presence provides a framework within which to illustrate Jesus' preaching and practice of love for one's enemies, and (3) whose tragic response to Jesus throws into relief the extent to which God goes to reclaim them (cf. Luke 19:41–44; 23:34).

223 C. K. Barrett. "Attitudes toward the Temple in the Acts of the Apostles." Pp. 345–67 in *Templum Amicitiae: Essays on the Second Temple Presented to Ernst Bammel*. Edited by W. Horbury. JSNTSS 48. Sheffield: JSOT Press, 1991.

Luke does not give a straightforward answer to the question, What attitude should Christians adopt toward the Jerusalem temple? As in his overall attitude toward Judaism, Luke seems to say to the temple both Yes and No, even if in the end the temple could only be destroyed since it could not become a Christian institution.

224 D. B. Gowler. *Host, Guest, Enemy and Friend: Portraits of the Pharisees in Luke and Acts*. Emory Studies in Early Christianity 2. New York/Bern/Frankfurt/Paris: Peter Lang, 1991.

An analysis of the characterization of the Pharisees in Luke-Acts that takes seriously the social dynamics of Luke's two volumes, noting both how the Pharisees are developed apart from the Jewish leadership as a group and the complexity of the Lukan portrayal, resulting in Acts' openness to and hope for the Pharisees.

225 J. B. Green. "The Demise of the Temple as 'Culture Center' in Luke-Acts: An Exploration of the Rending of the Temple Veil (Luke 23:44–49)." *Revue Biblique,* forthcoming. A revision of "The Death of Jesus and the Rending of the Temple Veil (Luke 23:44–49): A Window into Luke's Understanding of Jesus and the Temple." Pp. 543–57 in *Society of Biblical Literature 1991 Seminar Papers.* Edited by E. H. Lovering Jr. Atlanta: Scholars Press, 1991.

Attention to the socio-cultural significance of the temple in the narrative of Luke-Acts suggests that the torn veil at Jesus' crucifixion signifies the end of the temple as a sacred symbol of socio-religious power; as a consequence, the way has been opened fully to a mission to all people.

226 H. Räisänen. "The Redemption of Israel: A Salvation-Historical Problem in Luke-Acts." Pp. 94–114 in *Luke-Acts: Scandinavian Perspectives.* Edited by P. Luomanen. Publications of the Finnish Exegetical Society 54. Göttingen: Vandenhoeck & Ruprecht, 1991.

Argues, *contra* Tannehill (#44), that Luke no longer retains a lingering hope for the salvation of Israel through conversion. "Luke does have a salvation-historical problem which is not solvable in 'objectifying' terms. If God's old promises are fulfilled in Jesus, their content has been changed to such an extent as to be in effect nullified" (p. 110).

227 J. T. Sanders. "Who Is a Jew and Who Is a Gentile in the Book of Acts?" *NTS* 37 (1991): 434–55.

After a summary of the contemporary discussion on the relation of Luke-Acts to Judaism, against those who locate the author of Luke-Acts within Judaism and/or see him as a Jew, Sanders argues that Acts proposes that God had rejected the Jews.

228 C. H. Talbert. "Once Again: The Gentile Mission in Luke-Acts." Pp. 99–109 in *Der Treue Gottes Trauen: Beiträge zum Werk des Lukas für Gerhard Schneider*. Edited by C. Bussmann and W. Radl. Freiburg/Basel/Wien: Herder, 1991.

According to Acts, the Gentile mission originates both because of Jewish unbelief in accordance with the meaning of scriptural prophecy and because of Jewish unbelief due to failure to understand scriptural prophecy; this perspective would have been easily grasped within the cultural milieu of Luke's Mediterranean world and is an extension of the theme of status transposition set forth in the Gospel of Luke.

229 J. A. Darr. *On Character Building: The Reader and the Rhetoric of Characterization in Luke-Acts*, pp. 85–126. Literary Currents in Biblical Interpretation. Louisville: Westminster/John Knox, 1992.

Employing a literary approach, Darr argues that Luke presents the Pharisees as a "group character" noted above all for its imperceptiveness.

230 J. Jervell. "God's Faithfulness to the Faithless People: Trends in Interpretation of Luke-Acts." *Word and World* 12 (1992): 29–36.

Underscores the Jewishness of Luke-Acts, and argues that Luke testifies to the strength of Jewish Christianity in the last decades of the first century.

231 J. D. Kingsbury. "The Pharisees in Luke-Acts." Vol. 2, pp. 1497–512 in *The Four Gospels 1992: Festschrift Frans Neirynck*. Edited by F. Van Segbroeck. BETL 100. Leuven: Leuven University Press, 1992.

Calls into serious question the traditional view that Luke portrays the Pharisees in a relatively positive light so as to enlist their voice in the legitimation of Christianity.

232 J. B. Tyson. *Images of Judaism in Luke-Acts*. Columbia, S.C.: University of South Carolina Press, 1992.

The ambivalence of Luke's two-volume narrative toward the Jewish people and their religious life is designed to win support for the Christian movement (which embodies what is good of Judaism) among God-fearers, while indicating the superiority of Christianity over Judaism and explaining Jewish rejection of the Christian message.

5.6 Salvation, Salvation-History, and Eschatology

Conzelmann's *The Theology of St. Luke* (#37, #233) raised the issues which continue to be debated in these areas. His contention that Luke has substituted salvation history for expectation of an imminent parousia, though severely challenged, continues to spawn re-articulations on both sides of the issue as scholars continue to grapple with Luke's perspective on history, salvation-history, and eschatology. Additionally, the contention that Luke lacked a theology of the cross has occasioned numerous studies which seek to understand better the meaning of salvation in Luke-Acts.

233 H. Conzelmann. *The Theology of St. Luke* (esp. pp. 95–136). Translated by G. Buswell. London: Faber & Faber/New York: Harper & Row, 1960. Reprinted London: SCM/Philadelphia: Fortress, 1982. Original title: *Die Mitte der Zeit.* Tübingen: Mohr, 1953. Second edition: 1957.

Continuing to form the starting point for contemporary discussion of Lukan eschatology, though heavily contested, Conzelmann's main thesis is that Luke addressed the problem of the delayed parousia by a periodization of salvation-history in which Christ's coming is relegated to the distant future. The three epochs of redemptive history consist of the period of the Old Testament, the period of Jesus' earthly ministry, and the period of the church. In the epoch of the church the phenomenon of the Spirit is the substitute for "knowledge of the last things" and makes it unnecessary to know when they will take place.

234 H. J. Cadbury. "Acts and Eschatology." Pp. 300–321 in *The Background of the New Testament and Its Eschatology: In Honour of Charles Harold Dodd.* Edited by W. D. Davies and D. Daube. Cambridge: Cambridge University Press, 1954. Reprint: 1964.

In Acts, Luke corrects an overly expectant attitude toward the parousia, while at the same time strengthening the certainty of the final events of history.

235 R. H. Smith. "The Eschatology of Acts and Contemporary Exegesis." *Concordia Theological Monthly* 29 (1958): 641–63.

Divides a half century of scholarship into opposing schools; one school, including K. L. Schmidt, R. Bultmann, and P. Vielhauer, understands history and eschatology as diametrically opposed, thus, Luke is historicizing primitive eschatology; the other school, including E. Hoskyns, G. E. Wright, and C. H. Dodd, asserts God's revelation in and through history, hence, Luke views eschatology as inseparable from salvation history. A third position, represented by H. J. Cadbury, understands Luke's abbreviated treatment of future eschatology as evidence that it was taken for granted.

236 R. H. Smith. "History and Eschatology in Luke-Acts." *Concordia Theological Monthly* 29 (1958): 881–901.

Nuances the "symbiotic" relationship between history and eschatology generally, in the Christian era, and specifically, in the eschatology of Acts.

237 F. O. Francis. "Eschatology and History in Luke-Acts." *Journal of the American Academy of Religion* 37 (1969): 49–63.

Lukan eschatology must be understood on its own terms, not with reference to the Pauline or Johannine writings. By emphasizing the eschatological dimension in the ministries of Jesus, the seventy, the first generation, and second-generation Christians, Luke has achieved a profound synthesis of orderly, historical narrative and the eschatological truth of the church's teaching.

238 R. Zehnle. "The Salvific Character of Jesus' Death in Lucan Soteriology." *Theological Studies* 30 (1969): 420–44.

Examines Lukan soteriology and its relation to Jesus' death, concluding that Luke's soteriology is distinct from, but in no way inferior to, that of Paul. Luke does not use the doctrine of satisfaction to explain Jesus' death but emphasizes that by Christ's obedient life and death God's grace is made known.

239 E. Franklin. "The Ascension and the Eschatology of Luke-Acts." *Scottish Journal of Theology* 23 (1970): 191–200.

Luke's lack of emphasis on the parousia represents a reinterpretation rather than a reduction of such emphasis by early Christianity. Luke locates the full eschatological act in the ascension. This shapes Luke's interpretation of christology, discipleship, pneumatology, and soteriology. When the parousia comes "it also will be seen to take its place alongside those other events which he recounts as evidence for the Ascension and for the belief that Jesus is Lord" (p. 200). (See #176.)

240 S. G. Wilson. "Lucan Eschatology." *NTS* 15 (1970): 330–47.

Luke's eschatology did not relegate the parousia to a far distant and indefinite future, *contra* Conzelmann (#37). Rather, it has two strands, one which allows for a delay in the parousia and one which declares that the end will come soon. Because of Luke's practical, pastoral concerns, "Luke is treading a careful *via media,* at the same time both avoiding and correcting two false extremes" (p. 346).

241 E. E. Ellis. *Eschatology in Luke.* Philadelphia: Fortress, 1972.

Brief survey of introductory problems and scholarly opinion concerning Lukan eschatology, followed by Ellis' own articulation of a two-stage eschatology in dialogue with H. Conzelmann (#37), H. Flender (#100), and others.

242 R. H. Hiers. "The Problem of the Delay of the Parousia in Luke-Acts." *NTS* 20 (1974): 145–55.

Argues that Luke-Acts does not reflect the understanding of an extended church age. Rather, the church is living during the "the last days," characterized by the preaching of repentance, the outpouring of the Spirit, and the expectation of the kingdom.

243 W. J. Larkin Jr. "Luke's Use of the Old Testament as a Key to His Soteriology." *Journal of the Evangelical Theological Society* 20 (1977): 325–35.

Proposes the presence of Isaiah 53:12 in Luke 22:37 as the interpretive key for Luke's soteriology as understanding Jesus' death as vicarious atonement, and for a recognition of the Lukan passion as "interpretive midrash."

244 C. K. Barrett. "Theologia Crucis—in Acts?" Pp. 73–84 in *Theologia Crucis—Signum Crucis: Festschrift für Erich Dinkler zum 70. Geburtstag.* Edited by C. Andersen and G. Klein. Tübingen: Mohr, 1979.

The theology of the cross in Luke-Acts is expanded from the doctrine of the atonement to characterize the lifestyle of discipleship; thus, both a theology of the cross and a theology of glory are in evidence in Acts.

245 R. H. Fuller. "Luke and the Theologia Crucis." Pp. 214–20 in *Sin, Salvation, and the Spirit.* Edited by D. Durken. Collegeville, Minn.: Liturgical, 1979.

Contests the assertion that the cross in Luke's theology lacks soteriological significance by a comparison of key Lukan passages with Mark.

246 J. Kodell. "Luke's Theology of the Death of Jesus." Pp. 221–30 in *Sin, Salvation, and the Spirit.* Edited by D. Durken. Collegeville, Minn.: Liturgical, 1979.

As distinct from other New Testament writings, Luke's doctrine of salvific death finds emphasis in the "name" of the risen Lord who gives the Spirit. "The saving power of Jesus' name is the consequence of his exaltation, not directly of his death. But it is because of the kind of death he suffered that God raised him and, with him, all the lowly who would follow him to glory" (p. 229).

247 A. J. Mattill Jr. *Luke and the Last Things: A Perspective for the Understanding of Lukan Thought.* Dillsboro, N.C.: Western North Carolina Press, 1979.

Study of Lukan eschatological passages, underscoring their apocalyptic imagery and concluding that Luke's Gospel is written in expectation of an imminent parousia, to encourage believers to "push the end-time program" and hasten the day of the Lord.

248 K. Giles. "Present-Future Eschatology in the Book of Acts." *Reformed Theological Review* 40 (1981): 65–71; 41 (1982): 11–18.

A two-part series emphasizing future aspects of Lukan eschatology, such as the visible coming of the kingdom, Jesus' return, the resurrection of the dead, and the final judgment, as well as the present aspects of the church's experience at Pentecost and Spirit empowerment for mission. Concludes that Luke's dual emphases of present and future eschatology share more with Paul than is often asserted.

249 C. K. Barrett. "Salvation Proclaimed: Acts 4:8–12." *ExpTim* 94 (1982): 58–71.

Exposition of the significance of this text as the church's first post-resurrection proclamation of salvation exclusively in Jesus and in confrontation with Judaism.

250 B. R. Gaventa. "The Eschatology of Luke-Acts Revisited." *Encounter* 43 (1982): 27–42.

Reviews major positions and isolates dominant issues concerning Luke's eschatology which have emerged since Conzelmann (#37), underscoring that Luke has not relegated the promise of the parousia to the end of history. "Luke affirms that the parousia is a future fact and that its reality is to be affirmed in face of either doubt or apocalyptic speculation. The parousia is guaranteed by the promises which have already been fulfilled, the promise of the Spirit and the church's witness" (p. 42).

251 L. Sabourin. "The Eschatology of Luke." *BTB* 12 (1982): 73–76.

Sketches the main points of Lukan eschatology as well as the associated problems of the delay of the parousia, individualized eschatology, and Luke's "de-eschatologized" gospel.

252 K. Giles. "Salvation in Lucan Theology." *Reformed Theological Review* 42 (1983): 10–16, 45–49.

Two-part study of Luke's distinctive understanding of salvation in the domains of forgiveness, grace, word, spirit, and divine fellowship.

253 C. K. Barrett. "Faith and Eschatology in Acts 3." Pp. 1–17 in *Glaube und Eschatologie: Festschrift für Werner Georg Kümmel zum 80. Geburtstag.* Edited by E. Grasser and O. Merk. Tübingen: Mohr, 1985.

   Considers faith and eschatology in the healing of the lame beggar at the temple and in Peter's speech with attention to the Lukan understanding of the "name of Jesus" and to "individual eschatology."

254 R. J. Karris. "Luke's Soteriology of With-ness." *CTM* 12 (1985): 346–52.

   Considers Lukan soteriology through themes of union: in Jesus' table fellowship with sinners, through Jesus' calling individuals to communion with others, and of God with Jesus in his death as the suffering righteous one.

255 J. H. Neyrey. *The Passion According to Luke: A Redaction Study of Luke's Soteriology.* Theological Inquiries. New York/Mahwah: Paulist, 1985.

   Similar to Paul and Hebrews, Jesus' soteriological significance in Luke-Acts is viewed from the perspective of his role as the new Adam who does not succumb to temptation but ushers in salvation, reopening paradise. This salvation issues from a life of faith and obedience which climaxes in, yet is not limited to, Luke's passion account.

256 M. A. Plunkett. "Ethnocentricity and Salvation History in the Cornelius Episode." Pp. 465–79 in *Society of Biblical Literature 1985 Seminar Papers.* Edited by K. H. Richards. Atlanta: Scholars Press, 1985.

   Charts a major turning point in Lukan salvation history in its movement beyond the bounds of Judaism, abolishing the "ethnocentric character of the Christian mission," the "ethnocentric definition of the people of God," as well as the "ethnocentric definition of social patterns tied up with his previous relationship to Israel" (p. 478).

257 F. F. Bruce. "Eschatology in Acts." Pp. 51–63 in *Eschatology and the New Testament: Essays in Honor of George Raymond Beasley-Murray.* Edited by W. H. Gloer. Peabody, Mass.: Hendrickson, 1988.

Luke's perspective on the last things is explored through the themes of the restored kingdom, judgment and resurrection, expectation, and Gentile evangelization.

258 J. T. Carroll. *Response to the End of History: Eschatology and Situation in Luke-Acts.* Society of Biblical Literature Dissertation Series 92. Atlanta: Scholars Press, 1988.

In the Gospel of Luke salvation history and end-time expectation are united. Delay of the parousia undergirds rather than weakens expectation of the end; believers, informed by Scripture and Jesus' teaching, and anticipating the sudden yet certain consummation, are encouraged to live lives of alert, faithful obedience.

259 E. E. Ellis. "Eschatology in Luke Revisited." Pp. 296–303 in *L'Évangile de Luc—The Gospel of Luke.* Revised and enlarged edition of *L'Évangile de Luc: Problémes littéraires et théologiques.* BETL 32. Leuven: Leuven University Press, 1989.

A supplement to #241, updating the discussion on the problem of the delay of the parousia and distancing Lukan eschatology from Platonic conceptions.

260 J. B. Green. "'The Message of Salvation' in Luke-Acts." *Ex Auditu* 5 (1989): 21–34.

Salvation in Luke-Acts is characterized by reversal of positions, exemplified in Jesus' death and exaltation as God's Suffering Servant. "[M]ajor aspects of the Lukan message—including the means and content of salvation, the shape of discipleship and ethics, and eschatology—intersect at the junction of Luke's theology of the death of Jesus and his development of the salvation theme" (p. 23).

261 A. E. Nielsen. "The Purpose of the Lucan Writings with Special Reference to Eschatology." Pp. 76–93 in *Luke-Acts: Scandinavian Perspectives.* Edited by P. Luomanen. Publications of the Finnish Exegetical Society 54. Göttingen: Vandenhoeck & Ruprecht, 1991.

Concludes from a study of key Lukan texts and Eusebius that Luke-Acts does not reflect a radical shift in eschatological perspective nor does it indicate any underlying eschatological problems.

262 M. A. Powell. "Salvation in Luke-Acts." *Word and World* 12 (1992): 5–10.

Explores the meaning of "salvation" in Luke-Acts by charting each occurrence of its root and discussing its content, basis, and reception. Concludes that salvation for Luke is characterized by its availability to all, by participation in the reign of God, and by its present experience.

263 H. F. Bayer. "Christ-Centered Eschatology in Acts 3:17–26." Pp. 236–50 in *Jesus of Nazareth: Lord and Christ. Essays on the Historical Jesus and New Testament Christology.* Edited by J. B. Green and M. Turner. Grand Rapids: Eerdmans, 1994.

Contra Conzelmann (#233), Acts 3:17–26 suggests that Lukan eschatology is characterized by its christocentric basis rather than by a system of salvation-historical periods. Moreover, Luke's theology leaves intact a near expectation.

5.7 Discipleship and Mission

A wide variety of themes are included under the heading "Discipleship and Mission," a reflection of the wide-ranging interest Luke has in the matter of the human responses appropriate to God's gracious visitation in Jesus. People are called not only to embrace the call to discipleship but also to align themselves with God's purpose and to participate fully in a mission empowered by the Spirit. Especially prominent in recent discussion are (1) the nature of the church's mission, (2) the role of prayer, and (3) the Lukan teaching on possessions and the life of faith.

264 P. T. O'Brien. "Prayer in Luke-Acts." *TynB* 24 (1973): 111–27.

A survey of the importance of prayer in Luke's work, arguing that Luke especially highlights prayer as the means by which God directs salvation history in the ministry of Jesus and of the church.

265 S. S. Smalley. "Spirit, Kingdom and Prayer in Luke-Acts." *NovT* 15 (1973): 59–71.

"Luke . . . regards petitionary prayer as the means by which the dynamic power of God's Spirit is historically realised [sic] for purposes of salvation" (p. 68).

266 R. P. Martin. "Salvation and Discipleship in Luke's Gospel." *Int* 30 (1976): 366–80. Reprinted in *Interpreting the Gospels*, pp. 214–30. Edited by J. L. Mays. Philadelphia: Fortress, 1981.

A redaction-critical analysis of these two important themes of the Third Gospel.

267 L. T. Johnson. *The Literary Function of Possessions in Luke-Acts.* Society of Biblical Literature Dissertation Series 39. Missoula, Mont.: Scholars Press, 1977.

Argues that Luke-Acts manifests a dramatic pattern (i.e., "the story of the Prophet and the People") structuring the work as a whole, and that within this narrative possessions function symbolically.

268 R. J. Cassidy. *Jesus, Politics, and Society: A Study of Luke's Gospel.* Maryknoll, N.Y.: Orbis, 1978.

Demonstrates, against the background of the political leadership of Jesus' day, that Luke's Jesus was a significant threat to the social and political structures of the first-century world. (See also #94.)

269 A. A. Trites. "The Prayer Motif in Luke-Acts." Pp. 168–86 in *Perspectives on Luke-Acts.* Edited by C. H. Talbert. Danville, Va.: Association of Baptist Professors of Religion/ Edinburgh: T. & T. Clark, 1978.

Surveys the primary data on prayer in Luke and Acts, arguing that prayer is the means by which God directs redemptive history.

270 W. E. Pilgrim. *Good News to the Poor: Wealth and Poverty in Luke-Acts.* Minneapolis: Augsburg, 1981.

A wide-ranging examination of the Lukan material on wealth and poverty leading to the twin affirmations that the offer of the kingdom to the poor is a word of promise and hope, and that the rich share in this kingdom by virtue of their treatment of the poor and needy.

271 R. J. Cassidy and P. J. Scharper (eds.). *Political Issues in Luke-Acts.* Maryknoll, N.Y.: Orbis, 1983.

Carries on the line of discussion brought to the foreground in #268; includes essays by R. F. O'Toole, W. M. Swartley, J. D. M. Derrett, F. W. Danker, Q. Quesnell, J. M. Ford, C. H. Talbert, D. Schmidt, E. J. Via, and R. J. Cassidy.

272 L. T. Johnson. *Decision Making in the Church: A Biblical Model* (esp. pp. 46–87). Philadelphia: Fortress, 1983.

Examines the way that the process of making decisions is narrated in Acts 1:15–26; 4:23–31; 6:1–6; 9:26–30; 10:1–11:18; and 15:1–35 by way of suggesting how decision-making in the contemporary church might proceed from a biblical basis.

273 D. P. Seccombe. *Possessions and the Poor in Luke-Acts.* Studien zum Neuen Testament und seiner Umwelt B6. Linz: Fuchs, 1983.

Argues that, for Luke, "the poor" is Israel in its bondage and suffering at the hand of the wicked rulers of this age; Luke employs material on possessions and the poor, then, to present Jesus as the savior of Israel, "the poor."

274 D. P. Senior and C. Stuhlmueller. *The Biblical Foundations for Mission,* pp. 255–79. Maryknoll, N.Y.: Orbis, 1983.

The universal mission of the church is central to Luke's theology and he provides both a theological basis for that mission and wise instruction for those undertaking it.

275 J. M. Ford. *My Enemy Is My Guest: Jesus and Violence in Luke.* Maryknoll, N.Y.: Orbis, 1984.

Argues that Luke presents violent hopes of divine redemption in his birth narratives (Luke 1–2) so as to counter them by his presentation of a non-violent, enemy-loving Jesus.

276 J. A. Bergquist. "'Good News to the Poor': Why Does This Lucan Motif Appear to Run Dry in the Book of Acts?" *Bangalore Theological Forum* 18 (1986): 1–16.

The paucity of direct data regarding issues of wealth and poverty in Acts, especially *vis-à-vis* the Gospel of Luke, indicates that "good news to the poor" is not *the* dominant theological focus of Luke-Acts; this important motif is subordinated to the controlling theme of the announcement of God's universal salvation in Jesus.

277 B. R. Gaventa. *From Darkness to Light: Aspects of Conversion in the New Testament*, pp. 52–129. Overtures to Biblical Theology. Philadelphia: Fortress, 1986.

An examination of accounts of conversion within the fabric of the Lukan narrative reveals that, although Luke presents no paradigm for the experience of conversion in Luke-Acts, some themes are paramount. In particular, Luke's narrative underscores the prevenient role of God in conversion, the notion that conversions mark "beginnings" in Luke-Acts, and the reality that conversion takes place in the context of and has important ramifications for the experience of community.

278 M. V. Abraham. "Good News to the Poor in Luke's Gospel." *Bangalore Theological Forum* 19 (1987): 1–13. Reprinted in *Bible Bhashyam* 14 (1988): 65–77.

Underscores the importance of "the poor" to the message of Luke—rejecting any overly spiritualized notion of "poor" and asserting that discipleship for Luke is marked by faithfulness in the area of wealth; this faithfulness is best realized in communal sharing that embraces but also extends beyond the community of believers.

279 T. E. Schmidt. *Hostility to Wealth in the Synoptic Gospels*, pp. 135–62. JSNTSS 15. Sheffield: JSOT Press, 1987.

Argues that hostility to wealth is a fundamental tenet of every strata of the Synoptic tradition, irrespective of socio-economic conditions; the Gospel of Luke manifests a development of this hostile element beyond its appearance in Mark.

280 T. D'Sa. "The Salvation of the Rich in the Gospel of Luke." *Vidyajyoti* 52 (1988): 170–80.

For Luke, salvation is available to the rich too, provided they are awakened to their injustice to the poor and undergo conversion, imitating the example of Zacchaeus.

281 B. E. Beck. *Christian Character in the Gospel of Luke*. London: Epworth, 1989.

A thematic exploration of the "ideal of Christian character" supported by the composition of the Third Gospel.

282 J. R. Donahue. "Two Decades of Research on the Rich and Poor in Luke-Acts." Pp. 129–44 in *Justice and the Holy: Essays in Honor of Walter Harrelson.* Edited by D. A. Knight and P. J. Paris. Atlanta: Scholars Press, 1989.

Noting the importance of "the danger of riches and the proper use of the goods of the world" (p. 129) for Luke, Donahue focuses his survey on recent investigation of "the audience of Luke's teaching and the make-up of the community he addressed" (p. 136) as this relates to issues of poverty and wealth.

283 J. A. Fitzmyer. "Discipleship in the Lucan Writings." Pp. 117–45 in *Luke the Theologian: Aspects of His Teaching.* New York/Mahwah: Paulist, 1989.

Discusses the special religious sense of discipleship in early Christianity as well as Luke's portrait of Jesus' immediate disciples and Luke's demands of Christian commitment.

284 P. Pokornya. "Strategies of Social Formation in the Gospel of Luke." Pp. 106–18 in *Gospel Origins and Christian Beginnings: In Honor of James M. Robinson.* Edited by J. E. Goehring et al. Forum Fascicles 1. Sonoma, Calif.: Polebridge, 1990.

Luke, probably building on Qumranic and Hellenistic ideas, utilizes the models of eschatological exchange and compensation to advance his vision of social justice.

285 D. M. Sweetland. *Our Journey with Jesus: Discipleship According to Luke-Acts.* Good News Studies 23. Collegeville, Minn.: Liturgical, 1990.

A thematic exploration of discipleship in Luke-Acts, focusing on stories of call and commission, christology and discipleship, becoming a disciple, and the nature and role of the community of disciples.

286 J. Gillman. *Possessions and the Life of Faith: A Reading of Luke-Acts.* Zacchaeus Studies: New Testament. Collegeville, Minn.: Liturgical, 1991.

An excellent summary of the relationship between faith and wealth in Luke-Acts.

287 D. A. Neale. *None but the Sinners: Religious Categories in the Gospel of Luke.* JSNTSS 58. Sheffield: JSOT Press, 1991.

Argues that "sinners" are for the Gospel of Luke an indispensable ideological category by which Luke drives home his theology of transposition; against all expectations, "sinners" are "the saved."

288 S. F. Plymale. *The Prayer Texts of Luke-Acts.* American University Studies 7, Theology and Religion 118. New York: Peter Lang, 1991.

An examination of the prayer texts in Luke-Acts against the backdrop of contemporary understandings of prayer, leading to a synthetic analysis of Luke's theology of prayer, focusing on prayer as the means by which God guides and empowers his people; through prayer texts Luke communicates a divinely sanctioned understanding of salvation history.

289 J. O. York. *The Last Shall Be First: The Rhetoric of Reversal in Luke.* JSNTSS 46. Sheffield: JSOT Press, 1991.

An analysis of the double or "bi-polar" reversals (e.g., rich/poor) in the Third Gospel in order to understand their impact on our understanding of Lukan eschatology and how they might have shaped the values and responses of Luke's audience in the first-century world.

290 S. C. Barton. *The Spirituality of the Gospels,* pp. 71–112. London: SPCK, 1992.

Discusses major themes within Luke's understanding of spirituality, attempting to root spirituality in Luke's overall theology by emphasizing the nature of God's gracious initiative as portrayed by Luke and the kinds of response to that grace which together constitute Luke's conception of spirituality.

291 J. B. Green. "'Proclaiming Repentance and Forgiveness of Sins to All Nations': A Biblical Perspective on the Church's Mission." Pp. 13–43 in *The World Is My Parish: The Mission of the Church in Methodist Perspective.* Edited by A. G.

Padgett. Studies in the History of Missions 10. Lewiston, N.Y.: Edwin Mellen, 1992.

A study of programmatic pericopae in Luke and Acts leads to the conclusion that "where the Spirit is at work, the community of God's people, empowered by the Spirit, are showing the good news in ways that reflect Jesus' concern for the sick, the disadvantaged, the lost" (p. 43).

292 H. E. Dollar. *A Biblical-Missiological Exploration of the Cross-Cultural Dimensions in Luke-Acts.* San Francisco: Mellen Research University Press, 1993.

A reading of Luke-Acts through a missiological lens, asking, "Did Luke intentionally write his account of [the early Christian] movement from a cross-cultural standpoint?" (p. 2); cautions against treating Luke as a twentieth-century missiologist.

293 J. B. Green, "Good News to Whom? Jesus and the 'Poor' in the Gospel of Luke." Pp. 59–74 in *Jesus of Nazareth: Lord and Christ. Essays on the Historical Jesus and New Testament Christology.* Edited by J. B. Green and M. Turner. Grand Rapids: Eerdmans, 1994.

Argues that contemporary readings of "the poor" in the Third Gospel operate from too narrow and anachronistic a base, and that Luke's *economic* concerns must be integrated more fully into an understanding of the human condition and social interaction in Greco-Roman antiquity. The mission of Jesus is directed above all to "the poor" understood as those of low social status.

6

The Text of Luke-Acts

The Acts of the Apostles presents a special quandary for textual criticism because of its two disparate textual traditions, the Alexandrian and the Western. The latter is almost ten percent longer than the former, and the character of each is distinctive. This has given rise to a number of explanations—especially (1) that both text forms derive from the same author, or (2) that one preserves the more original and the other a deliberate revision. (Cf. the essay by P. Head in #372.)

294 J. H. Ropes. *The Text of Acts.* Vol. 3 of *The Beginnings of Christianity,* Part One: *The Acts of the Apostles.* Edited by F. J. Foakes-Jackson and K. Lake. London: Macmillan, 1926. Reprint: Grand Rapids: Baker, 1979.

A lengthy discussion of issues related to the history and reconstruction of the text of Acts (arguing, in part, that the Western text is a rewriting of the original by someone other than Luke), followed by the text, apparatus, and textual notes.

295 A. F. J. Klijn. *A Survey of the Researches into the Western Text of the Gospels and Acts.* Utrecht: Drukkerij, 1949.

A survey of research on the Western Text from 1881 to the year of publication.

296 M. Dibelius. "The Text of Acts: An Urgent Critical Task."
Translated by P. Schubert. Pp. 84–92 in *Studies in the Acts
of the Apostles*. Edited by H. Greeven. London: SCM/New
York: Charles Scribner's Sons, 1956. Original title: "Der
Text der Apostelgeschichte." Pp. 76–83 in *Aufsätze zur
Apostelgeschichte*. FRLANT 60. Göttingen: Vandenhoeck
& Ruprecht, 1951. Second edition: 1953.

> The history of the transmission of the text of Acts prior
> to its incorporation into the New Testament distin-
> guishes the problem of the text of Acts from that of the
> Gospels and Letters. The Western text has no claim to
> originality, though it may contain superior readings at
> some points.

297 P. H. Menoud. "The Western Text and the Theology of
Acts." *Society for New Testament Studies Bulletin* 2 (1951):
19–32. Reprinted in Menoud's *Jesus Christ and the Faith: A
Collection of Studies by Phillipe H. Menoud*, pp. 61–83.
Translated by E. M. Paul. Pittsburgh Theological Mono-
graph Series 18. Pittsburgh: Pickwick, 1978.

> The Western text overall is secondary; its "writer" pre-
> serves the original text when it suits the writer's pur-
> poses, but otherwise modernizes it by way of making it
> more intelligible to "his age."

298 A. F. J. Klijn. "A Survey of the Researches into the Western
Text of the Gospels and Acts (1949–59)." *NovT* 3 (1959): 1–
27, 161–73.

> A supplement to #295; surveys scholarship on the text
> during this ten-year period, indicating the degree to
> which a wider range of influences on the development of
> textual traditions were studied.

299 E. J. Epp. *The Theological Tendency of Codex Bezae Cant-
abrigiensis in Acts*. SNTSMS 3. Cambridge: Cambridge
University Press, 1966.

> Segregating questions of origin or originality, this study
> examines the D text of Acts on its own terms as a theo-
> logical document, leading to the conclusion that Codex
> Bezae has a distinctive anti-Judaic tendency.

300 A. F. J. Klijn. *A Survey of the Researches into the Western Text of the Gospels and Acts: Part Two* (1949–69) (esp. pp. 56–65). NovTSup 21. Leiden: Brill, 1969.

Concludes that (1) "the riddle of the Western Text in Acts has not been solved" (p. 64) and (2) that the eclectic method for ascertaining the original text of Acts seems to be the right method.

301 B. M. Metzger. *A Textual Commentary on the Greek New Testament: A Companion Volume to the United Bible Societies' Greek New Testament (Third Edition)*, pp. 259–72. London/New York: United Bible Societies, 1971.

An introductory survey of the historical debate, noting that the UBS Greek New Testament, 3d edition, generally prefers the Alexandrian text.

302 M. Wilcox. "Luke and the Bezan Text in Acts." Pp. 447–55 in *Les Actes des Apôtres: Traditions, Rédaction, Théologie.* Edited by J. Kremer. BETL 48. Leuven: Leuven University Press, 1979.

The Western text contains a surprising number of apparent Lukan tendencies; the D-text and B-text are probably two distinct revisions of the one original Lukan text.

303 M.-É. Boismard. "The Text of Acts: A Problem of Literary Criticism?" Pp. 147–57 in *New Testament Textual Criticism.* Edited by E. J. Epp and G. D. Fee. Oxford: Oxford University Press, 1981.

Building on #302, attempts to demonstrate that the Western text has an undeniable Lukan style.

304 M.-É. Boismard and A. Lamouille. *Le Texte Occidental des Actes des Apôtres: Reconstitution et Réhabilitation.* 2 vols. Paris: Recherche sur les Civilisations, 1984.

Includes a lengthy discussion of the history of the study of the Western text of Acts, a presentation of the Western and Alexandrian texts of Acts, an apparatus dealing above all with variants between these two textual traditions, and an examination of the Lukanisms in each textual tradition.

305 R. S. MacKenzie. "The Western Text of Acts: Some Lucanisms in Selected Sermons." *JBL* 104 (1985): 637–50.

Locates Lukanisms in the D textual tradition of selected
missionary sermons in Acts and concludes that the Bezan
text may have preserved elements of a textual tradition
that is more Lukan than the present B-type text.

306 R. F. Hull Jr. "'Lucanisms' in the Western Text of Acts? A
Reappraisal." *JBL* 107 (1988): 695–707.
A response to #305, insisting that the existence of Lukan
style in the D-type text of Acts leads to no clear conclusions about the relative originality of this text over the
B-type; also identifies certain past hypotheses for explaining the two types of text for Acts as failures.

307 T. C. Greer Jr. "The Presence and Significance of Lucanisms
in the 'Western' Text of Acts." *JSNT* 39 (1990): 59–76.
A critical, cautionary assessment of recent work on the
Western text (including ##302, 303, 304, 305), focusing
on the presence of alleged Lukanisms in the Western text
of Acts.

308 C. D. Osburn. "The Search for the Original Text of Acts:
The International Project on the Text of Acts." *JSNT* 44
(1991): 39–55.
Asserts that there is still very little agreement on the nature of the original text of Acts and underscores the necessity of the production of a critical edition of the text of
Acts.

309 W. A. Strange. *The Problem of the Text of Acts.* SNTSMS
71. Cambridge: Cambridge University Press, 1992.
Provides a helpful review of research on the problem of
the Western text of Acts; theorizes that Luke died before
completing the Book of Acts, and his posthumous editors
left two versions of Acts now represented by the two
manuscript traditions.

Part 2

Luke-Acts
and Ancient
Historiography

7

The History and Nature of Historiography

The entire question of the history and nature of historiography has been problematized by the post-modern milieu and the continued debate concerning the relation and adequacy of a narrative representation of historical reality. The modern scientific worldview of history which once accused ancient historiographical methods of naiveté, partiality, and distortion has itself become incriminated in the post-modern epoch. The twentieth century's fascination and ongoing debate over the nature of language and particularly narrative is reflected in the present state of flux in our understanding of history. The linguistic, aesthetic, ideological, and social forces which come to bear on the configuration and interpretation of history have not been fully integrated within the discipline. The following titles are mere suggestions for an entry point to this ongoing debate.

310 E. Auerback. *Mimesis: The Representation of Reality in Western Literature.* Translated by W. R. Trask. Princeton: Princeton University Press, 1953. Original title: *Mimesis: Dargestellte Wirklichkeit in der abendländischen Literature.* Berne: A. Francke, 1946. Reprinted Garden City, N.Y.: Doubleday, 1957.

A far-ranging exploration of "the representation of reality
in western literature" and its characterization in terms of
the historical consciousness of each era, with implications for the literary study of biblical historical narratives. Auerbach's treatment of biblical texts such as Genesis and Mark was one of the first to evoke the narrative's
literary qualities, without predisposition as to their historicity.

311 M. A. Fitzsimmons et al. (eds.). *The Development of Historiography.* Harrisburg, Pa.: Stackpole, 1954. Reprinted Port
Washington, N.Y.: Kennikat Press, 1967.

A general introduction to the development of historiography covering Near Eastern, Early and Late Greek, Roman,
and early Christian historiography; with a very basic
methodological introduction raising questions of dis-
agreement, presuppositions, ideology, and objectivity.

312 A. W. Mosley. "Historical Reporting in the Ancient World."
NTS (1965–66): 10–26.

Examines Greek, Roman, and Jewish historical works to
determine their criteria for historiography and their faithfulness to their own canons, contending that many writers were concerned with historical accuracy and authen-
ticity, hence we must not assume in advance that writers
of the New Testament were not.

313 H. White. *Metahistory: The Historical Imagination in
Nineteenth-Century Europe* (esp. pp. 1–42). Baltimore/Lon-
don: Johns Hopkins University Press, 1973.

A foundational work for those who underscore the poetic,
aesthetic, or rhetorical aspects of historiography, or what
the historian *does* with the facts. White identifies several
levels inherent in narrative historiography beyond mere
chronicle including mode of emplotment (drawing upon
N. Frye's typology of plots), mode of argument (utilizing
the work of S. Pepper), mode of ideological implication
(applying the analysis of K. Mannheim), and the mode of
poetic language itself (employing the four basic tropes).

314 P. Ricoeur. "The Narrative Function." *Semeia* 13 (1978):
177–202.

Sophisticated yet accessible outline of a general theory of narrative—both historical and fictional. In *form*, both historical and fictional narrative share story configuration and emplotment, but at the level of *reference* historical narrative refers to events outside the narrative while fiction does not. "But both historical and fictional narratives have in common an intersecting reference, a reference to historicity, to the fundamental fact that we make our history and are historical beings" (p. 177). Concludes that "history opens us to the possible, while fiction . . . brings us back to the essential" (p. 198). (For a full development of Ricoeur's theory of narrative cf. *Time and Narrative*. 3 vols. Chicago/London: University of Chicago Press, 1984–88.)

315 H. White. *Tropics of Discourse: Essays on Cultural Criticism.* Baltimore/London: Johns Hopkins University Press, 1978.

Deriving its title from the rhetorical *trope* or figure of speech, this collection of twelve essays addresses the metahistorical level of *historiographical styles.* That is, the figuration of all discourse, fictional and historical, as a process "that is more tropical than logical" (p. 1). Or, the process whereby "all discourse constitutes the objects which it pretends only to describe realistically and to analyze objectively" (p. 2).

316 M. Krieger (ed.). *The Aims of Representation: Subject/Text/History.* Irvine Studies in the Humanities. New York: Columbia University Press, 1987. Reprinted Palo Alto: Stanford University Press, 1993.

Collection of essays locating the topic of the representation of historical reality within the recent sequence of theoretical focal points of: "subject" or author-controlled text theory, "text" or the work in the larger matrix of textuality, and "history" or the work as produced and absorbed by "power-driven historical forces."

317 H. White. *The Content of the Form: Narrative Discourse and Historical Representation* (esp. pp. 1–57, 169–213). Baltimore/London: Johns Hopkins University Press, 1987.

A collection of eight essays addressing the problem of the relation between narrative discourse and historical representation, including such topics as objectivity and moralizing in ancient and modern historical accounts, the typologies of modern historical theory, and questions of method and ideology.

318 N. Carroll. "Interpretation, History and Narrative." *Monist* 73 (1990): 134–66.

An assessment and critique of H. White's (##313, 315, 317) metahistorical theory and its implications for the philosophy of history, suggesting that "the reduction of all narrative to the status of fiction seems a desperate and inevitably self-defeating way in which to grant the literary dimension of historiography its due" (p. 162).

319 B. Stock. *Listening for the Text: On the Uses of the Past.* Baltimore: Johns Hopkins University Press, 1990.

An insightful discussion of the ways in which communities give shape to the past by their preferences for one type of retrospection over another—already *before* the work of "official interpreters" commences. The study of history, then, is interested not only in "what actually happened," but also in what people "thought was taking place, and the ways in which their feelings, perceptions, and narratives influenced or were influenced by the events they experienced" (p. 16).

8

Old Testament and Jewish-Hellenistic Historiography

Increasingly Luke-Acts is being explored within the context of the Jewish-Hellenistic environment and as the work of a Jewish-Hellenistic historiographer. Luke evinces an extensive knowledge of the Greek Old Testament including the Apocrypha, and the Jewish historiographer Josephus has long been considered his contemporary in many regards. Below are listed a cross section of influences, ancient and first century, which informed the Jewish-Hellenistic context from which, and of which, Luke wrote. (See also ##70, 78.)

320 R. C. Dentan (ed.). *The Idea of History in the Ancient Near East* (esp. pp. 99–131). American Oriental Series 38. New Haven: Yale, 1955. Reprinted 1966.

   Well-integrated series of Yale symposium papers including the topics of "Ancient Israel," "The Hellenistic Orient," and "Earliest Christianity."

321 H. W. Attridge. *The Interpretation of Biblical History in the Antiquitates Judaicae of Flavius Josephus.* Harvard Dissertations in Religion 7. Missoula, Mont.: Scholars Press, 1976.

Exemplifies the fact that Josephus, though also a Jewish theological thinker, intentionally followed Greek historiographical models such as Dionysius of Halicarnassus.

322 N. Wyatt. "The Old Testament Historiography of the Exilic Period." *Studia Theologica* 3 (1979): 45–67.

Argues that neither Israel's understanding of God's actions in history nor its non-cyclical view of history is unique in the ancient Near East. Also asserts that neither the Deuteronomic history nor the Priestly history may be classified as *history*, strictly speaking, but as interpretations which stand over against history.

323 R. T. France. "Jewish Historiography, Midrash, and the Gospels." Pp. 99–127 in *Gospel Perspectives*, Vol. 3: *Studies in Midrash and Historiography*. Edited by R. T. France and D. Wenham. Sheffield: JSOT Press, 1983.

Questions the alleged prevalence of "creative midrash" in first-century Jewish historiography, suggesting that such midrashic activity is not characteristic of Jewish historiography nor should it be viewed as determinative of New Testament historiography.

324 T. E. Fretheim. *Deuteronomic History.* Interpreting Biblical Texts. Nashville: Abingdon, 1983.

Accessible introduction to the Deuteronomic history with an apt treatment of historiography.

325 C. R. Holladay. *Fragments from Hellenistic Jewish Authors,* Vol. 1: *Historians.* Society of Biblical Literature Texts and Translations 20. Chico, Calif.: Scholars Press, 1983.

Compiles in one volume the writings of Hellenistic Jewish historians to meet the need of "a collection which provides in accessible form the Greek text, critical apparatus, English translation, introductory material to each author, including bibliography, and annotations to the translation" (p. xii).

326 T. Rajak. *Josephus: The Historian and His Society.* Philadelphia: Fortress/London: Duckworth, 1983. Reprinted 1984.

Excellent introduction, in conjunction with Attridge (#321), to Josephus and his account of the Roman-Jewish

War, asserting his basic reliability as a historian who participated in the events he recorded.

327 J. van Seeters. *In Search of History: Historiography in the Ancient World and the Origins of Biblical History.* New Haven/London: Yale University Press, 1983.

Introduces ancient historiography in the Near East in general and in Israel in particular while challenging common assumptions concerning Israel and historiography in antiquity. Maintains a late date for the beginning of the historiographical writing in Israel and contends that a comparison with Greek history is at least as important as Near Eastern comparisons.

328 H. W. Attridge. "Jewish Historiography." Pp. 311–43 in *Early Judaism and Its Modern Interpreters.* The Bible and Its Modern Interpreters 2. Edited by R. A. Kraft and G. W. Nickelsburg. Philadelphia: Fortress/Atlanta: Scholars Press, 1986.

Valuable introduction, with extensive bibliography, to the field of the study of Jewish historiography since World War II; sensitive to the cultural and literary development of the period.

329 S. J. D. Cohen. "History and Historiography in the *Against Apion* of Josephus." *History and Theory* 27 (1988): 1–11. Reprinted in *Essays in Jewish Historiography,* pp. 1–11. South Florida Studies in the History of Judaism 15. Edited by A. Rapoport-Albert. Atlanta: Scholars Press, 1991.

Discusses Josephus' practice of Greek historical criticism which he employed in all his works but particularly in *Against Apion,* his fullest statement on history and historiography.

330 B. Halpern. *The First Historians: The Hebrew Bible and History.* San Francisco: Harper & Row, 1988.

Pace Noth, this study of the Deuteronomistic history intends "to determine what ancient Israelite historians thought history demanded, to illuminate the discipline to which they subjected themselves. The thesis of this volume is that some of these authors . . . had authentic antiquarian intentions. They meant to furnish fair and accurate representations of Israelite antiquity" (p. 3).

331 R. G. Hall. *Revealed Histories: Techniques for Ancient Jewish and Christian Historiography.* Journal for the Study of the Pseudepigrapha Supplement Series 6. Sheffield: JSOT Press, 1991.

Highlighting a neglected aspect of Jewish and Christian historical consciousness which expected the "best history" to be based on revelation, Hall surveys Jewish and Christian literature between 200 B.C.E. and 130 C.E. for examples of revealed history and its use as a rhetorical, epistemological, and hermeneutical technique.

332 K. A. D. Smelik. "The Use of the Hebrew Bible as a Historical Source." Pp. 1–34 in *Converting the Past: Studies in Ancient Israelite and Moabite Historiography.* Oudtestamentlische Studiën 28. Leiden: Brill, 1992.

Provides, within the context of Israelite historiography as a historical source, an accessible overview of historiographical method and genres of the ancient Near East.

9

Greco-Roman Historiography

Any assessment of Luke as a historian must consider the understanding of the nature and purpose of historiography in antiquity. Though a pioneer in many ways, Luke as an educated member of the Greco-Roman society was undoubtedly influenced by the ideals and institutions of his day. An understanding of such, both contemporary and from the perspectives of antiquity, is prerequisite for a comprehension of Luke's agenda. (For the importance of speeches in Greek historiography, see also §10.3.4.)

333 *Dionysius of Halicarnassus. The Critical Essays. Vols. I and II*, with an English Translation. Translated by E. Cary. Loeb Classical Library. Cambridge, Mass.: Harvard University Press, 1974.

> Dionysius of Halicarnassus, a Greek historian and rhetoric teacher, taught in Rome between 30 and 8 B.C.E. His works, published near the end of the first century B.C.E., critiqued other historians and expounded on the relationship between historiography and rhetoric. His *Roman Antiquities*, in twenty volumes, served as the model for Josephus' *Antiquities of the Jews*, also in twenty volumes. (See ##73, 360.)

334 Lucian. *How to Write History*, in *Lucian*, with an English Translation. Translated by A. M. Harmon. Loeb Classical Library. Cambridge, Mass.: Harvard University, 1959.

Lucian (*ca.* 120–*ca.* 200 C.E.), a Greek satirist and rhetorician, satirizes his lesser known contemporaries' attempts to emulate such great historians as Thucydides, Herodotus, and Xenophon, as well as includes his own judgments on the proper nature of historiography in one of the most significant discussions of the practice from antiquity.

335 J. N. Bury. *The Ancient Greek Historians*. London: Macmillan, 1909. Reprinted New York: Dover Publications, 1958.

Historical survey of Greek historiography to the first century B.C.E., its influence on Roman historians, as well as ancient historiographers' own reflections on the purpose of historiography.

336 H. Bengston. *Introduction to Ancient History*. Translated by R. I. Frank and F. D. Gilliard. Berkeley: University of California Press, 1970. Original title: *Einführung in die alte Geschichte*. Munich: C. H. Beck, 1949–1969.

A fundamental overview and introduction to the discipline of ancient historiography including: Bibliography, History of the Study of Antiquity, Chronology, Geography, Anthropology, Sources, Epigraphy, Papyrology, and Numismatics.

337 E. Badian. "The Early Historians." Pp. 1–38 in *Latin Historians*. Edited by T. A. Dorey. New York: Basic Books/London: Routledge and Kegan Paul, 1966.

Briefly traces the development of the forms and traditions of Roman historiography up to the age of Cicero (106–43 B.C.E.).

338 A. Momigliano. *Studies in Historiography*. New York: Harper and Row/London: Weidenfeld & Nicolson, 1966.

Collection of thirteen essays devoted to the "disciplined interpretation" of Greek and Roman historians, as well as the history of historiography with frequent attention to method.

339 M. Grant. *The Ancient Historians.* New York: Scribner/ London: Weidenfeld and Nicolson, 1970.

Panoramic introduction to the Greek and Latin historians, covering Near Eastern and Greek backgrounds in addition to the background and methodology of individual historians.

340 T. S. Brown. *The Greek Historians.* Lexington, Mass.: D. C. Heath, 1973.

Focuses less on the individual historians of antiquity as on the important changes occurring in the discipline from the earliest fragmentary picture of the "pre-historians" to the time of the Roman conquest.

341 H. F. Harding. *The Speeches of Thucydides.* Lawrence, Kan.: Coronado, 1973.

A collection of the speeches of Thucydides from *The History of the Peloponnesian War* exemplifying the importance of speeches in the development of Thucydides' account and in Greek historiography as a rule. Includes an introduction to the context and chronology for each speech.

342 C. W. Fornarna. *The Nature of History in Ancient Greece and Rome.* Berkeley: University of California Press, 1983.

General introduction to the *field* of ancient historiography, covering the genre of history and its relations to other genres, ancient methodology and theoretical foundations, and the significant role of the speech in ancient historiography.

10

Luke as Historiographer

For the past century Lukan scholars have been engaged in a persistent debate regarding Luke's value as a historian of the life of the earliest Christian communities. One side has tended to characterize Luke's intentions as theological or literary to the exclusion of objective historiography. The other has inclined toward a defensive position, emphasizing Luke's validity as a historian by the standards of the day and as corroborated by other ancient sources and archeological data. In between are a spectrum of positions which would mediate or synthesize facets of this debate.

10.1 Luke as Historian: General Discussions and Archaeological Evidence

343 M. Dibelius. "The Acts of the Apostles as an Historical Source." Pp. 102–8 in *Studies in the Acts of the Apostles.* Edited by H. Greeven. Translated by M. Ling. London: SCM/ New York: Charles Scribner's Sons, 1956. Original title: "Die Apostelgeschichte als Geschichtsquelle." Pp. 91–95 in *Aufsätze zur Apostelgeschichte.* FRLANT 60. Göttingen: Vandenhoeck & Ruprecht, 1951. Second edition: 1953.

In evaluating Acts as an historical document, the first question is what Luke's intentions were and what means were available to him. Luke wanted to portray God's leadership of the church within the framework of its history and he did so by arranging and illuminating current accounts he had gathered.

344 M. Dibelius. "The Acts of the Apostles in the Setting of the History of Early Christian Literature." Pp. 192–206 in *Studies in the Acts of the Apostles*. Edited by H. Greeven. Translated by M. Ling. London: SCM/New York: Charles Scribner's Sons, 1956. Original title: "Die Apostelgeschichte in Rahmen der urchristlichen Literaturgeschichte." Pp. 163–74 in *Aufsätze zur Apostelgeschichte*. FRLANT 60. Göttingen: Vandenhoeck & Ruprecht, 1951. Second edition: 1953.

Acts is distinguished from the rest of the New Testament by its consciously literary character, and from other historical works by its theological intent. Its literary purpose has effected both the selection and shaping of its sources, implying an "epoch" in early Christian writing.

345 M. Dibelius. "The First Christian Historian." Pp. 123–37 in *Studies in the Acts of the Apostles*. Edited by H. Greeven. Translated by M. Ling. London: SCM/New York: Charles Scribner's Sons, 1956. Original title: "Der erste christliche Historiker." Pp. 108–19 in *Aufsätze zur Apostelgeschichte*. FRLANT 60. Göttingen: Vandenhoeck & Ruprecht, 1951. Second edition: 1953.

Historians not only gather and frame traditions, but also seek to articulate the meaning of the events portrayed. This Luke has done while at the same time proclaiming faith in Christ.

346 C. K. Barrett. *Luke the Historian in Recent Study*. London: Epworth, 1961. Reprinted 1982.

A succinct survey of the state of Lukan studies, assessing the theological issues behind Luke's historical form in dialogue with the leading scholarship of the day, including the works of M. Dibelius (#36), H. Conzelmann (#37), and E. Haenchen (#29).

347 E. Haenchen. "The Book of Acts as Source Material for the History of Early Christianity." Pp. 258–78 in *Studies in Luke-Acts* (P. Schubert Festschrift). Edited by L. E. Keck and J. L. Martyn. Nashville: Abingdon, 1966.

Throughout Acts edification rather than historical reliability is of central concern. The book of Acts may serve as source material for the history of early Christianity "only if the reader frees himself [sic] from the charm of its simplified presentation and does not overlook the thread of what is edifying in the Lucan fabric" (p. 265).

348 W. W. Gasque. "The Historical Value of the Book of Acts: An Essay in the History of New Testament Criticism." *Evangelical Quarterly* 41 (1969): 68–88.

Beginning with De Wette and Baur, traces the historical background of the radically negative stance toward the historical value of Acts reflected in German scholarship. This stance is criticized for its basis on a tradition of criticism rather than on "a careful study of the text of Acts itself in the context of the historical setting of the Graeco-Roman world" (p. 87).

349 B. Van Elderen. "Some Archaeological Observations on Paul's First Missionary Journey." Pp. 151–61 in *Apostolic History and the Gospel: Biblical and Historical Essays Presented to F. F. Bruce on His 60th Birthday*. Edited by W. W. Gasque and R. P. Martin. Grand Rapids: Eerdmans/Exeter: Paternoster, 1970.

Discusses archaeological data relevant to the identification of Sergius Paulus (Acts 13:7) and the site of Derbe (Acts 14:6, etc.).

350 W. W. Gasque. "The Historical Value of the Book of Acts: The Perspective of British Scholarship." *Theologische Zeitschrift* 28 (1972): 177–96.

Highlights, by way of a survey of the contributions of British scholars J. B. Lightfoot, W. M. Ramsay, and F. F. Bruce, the near consensus among British scholarship for the historical reliability of Acts over against the extreme skepticism of German scholarship.

351 C. J. Hemer. "Paul at Athens: A Topographical Note." *NTS* 20 (1974): 341–50.

Paul's Areopagus address in Acts 17:16–34 need not have taken place on the hill but in a court such as the *Stoa*

Basileos excavated north of the Agora. This setting accords well with the narrative in Acts.

352 C. J. Hemer. "Alexandria Troas." *TynB* 26 (1975): 79–112.
Employs a detailed archaeological and geographical description of this overlooked city to accentuate the strategic role it played in the dissemination of Christianity and how several "New Testament critical problems" may be clarified by such study.

353 C. J. Hemer. "Euraquilo and Melita." *JTS* n.s. 26 (1975): 100–111.
Contends, *contra* A. Acworth, for the traditional identification of Melita as Malta for the location of Paul's shipwreck on the basis of textual, geographical, navigational, ethnographical, and zoological arguments.

354 C. J. Hemer. "The Adjective 'Phrygia.'" *JTS* n.s. 27 (1976): 122–26.
Asserts that "Phrygia" in Paul's itinerary in Acts 16:6 should be read as an adjective, following W. Ramsay, on the basis of its occurrence in texts between 400 B.C.E. and 400 C.E.

355 C. J. Hemer. "Luke the Historian." *BJRL* 60 (1977): 28–51.
Addresses the need to assess Luke's value as a historian by his performance rather than by the intricacies of ancient historiography, as well as the necessity of framing interpretive questions in light of all available data. Concludes that Luke-Acts was composed before 70 C.E. by a companion of Paul close to the events found in the latter half of Acts.

356 C. J. Hemer. "Phrygia: A Further Note." *JTS* n.s. 28 (1977): 99–101.
Further literary and epigraphic examples which confirm Hemer's previous findings (#354) that "Phrygia" in Paul's itinerary in Acts 16:6 should be read as an adjective.

357 W. W. Gasque. "The Book of Acts and History." Pp. 54–72 in *Unity and Diversity in New Testament Theology: Essays in Honor of George Eldon Ladd.* Edited by R. A. Guelich. Grand Rapids: Eerdmans, 1978.

A defense of Acts' historical reliability in the areas of modern historical research, alleged free invention in the speeches, and P. Vielhauer's "Paulinisms" (#468).

358 F. F. Bruce. "St. Paul in Macedonia." *BJRL* 61 (1978–79): 337–54.

The record of Paul's journey through Macedonia in Acts 16:6–18:5 reflects Luke's accuracy in recording its political organization in 50 C.E.

359 M. Hengel. *Acts and the History of Earliest Christianity.* Translated by J. Bowden. London: SCM/Philadelphia: Fortress, 1979. Original title: *Zur urchristlichen Geschichtsschreibung.* Stuttgart: Calwer, 1979.

Attempts a balance between radical historical skepticism and the rejection of the historical-critical method. Based on the nature of ancient historiography and the reliability of its sources, Acts is a reliable source for constructing a history of early Christianity, which is outlined in the latter half of the study.

360 W. C. van Unnik. "Luke's Second Book and the Rules of Hellenistic Historiography." Pp. 37–60 in *Les Actes des Apôtres: Traditions, Rédaction, Théologie.* Edited by J. Kremer. BETL 48. Leuven: Leuven University Press, 1979.

When evaluated against the criteria for historiography set forth by Dionysius of Halicarnassus and Lucian (see above ##333, 334), Acts appears as a competent illustration of ancient historiography.

361 M. Hengel. "Luke the Historian and the Geography of Palestine in the Acts of the Apostles." Translated by J. Bowden. Pp. 97–128 in *Between Jesus and Paul: Studies in the History of Earliest Christianity.* Philadelphia: Fortress, 1983. Original title: "Der Historiker Lukas und die Geographie Palästinas in der Apostelgeschichte." *Zeitschrift des Deutschen Palästinavereins* 98 (1983).

Modifies the view that Luke was completely ignorant of the geography of Palestine. Rather, Luke viewed the whole country from the perspective of someone who comes from abroad—well acquainted with some regions while possessing a more general understanding of others.

362 E. Richard. "Luke—Writer, Theologian, Historian: Research and Orientation of the 1970s." *BTB* 13 (1983): 3–15.

Includes a helpful synopsis of 1970s scholarship assessing the relationship of Luke-Acts to Greco-Roman historiography.

363 D. L. Balch. "Acts as Hellenistic Historiography." Pp. 429–32 in *Society of Biblical Literature 1985 Seminar Papers.* Edited by K. H. Richards. Atlanta: Scholars Press, 1985.

Critical response to D. Schmidt (#365) suggesting that some first-century readers or hearers of Acts may have had a greater knowledge of Hellenistic rather than Deuteronomistic history. Hence, in the reading of Acts they may have heard the divine pattern of "prophecy and fulfillment" of Dionysius of Halicarnassus' *Roman Antiquities* rather than that of Deuteronomistic history.

364 F. F. Bruce. "The Acts of the Apostles: Historical Record or Theological Reconstruction?" *ANRW* 2.25.3:2569–603 (1985).

After a consideration of the contents of Acts, its historicity regarding general facts, the speeches, Luke's sources, and other introductory questions, proposes that because Luke was "a good theologian as well as a good historian, he did not allow his theology to distort his history" (p. 2603).

365 D. Schmidt. "The Historiography of Acts: Deuteronomistic or Hellenistic?" Pp. 417–27 in *Society of Biblical Literature 1985 Seminar Papers.* Edited by K. H. Richards. Atlanta: Scholars Press, 1985.

On the basis of converging scholarship since H. J. Cadbury, the promise-fulfillment pattern of Acts, and an examination of the historiography of the Deuteronomistic tradition, this prolegomenon for a fuller investigation of the basis of the historiography of Acts concludes that Acts is derived from Deuteronomistic historiography.

366 F. F. Bruce. "The First Church Historian." Pp. 1–14 in *Church, Word, and Spirit: Historical and Theological Essays in Honor of Geoffrey W. Bromiley.* Edited by J. E Bradley and R. A. Muller. Grand Rapids: Eerdmans, 1987.

Luke, as a true pioneer in the writing of the history of the primitive church, followed the well established genre of *history* for his account. This is made evident by comparing Acts to the historiographical standards of the day, such as Lucian's *How to Write History* (#334), as well as a consideration of Luke's sources, Acts' speeches, Luke-Acts' accuracy in regard to world history, and Acts' relation to Paul's letters.

367 C. J. Hemer. *The Book of Acts in the Setting of Hellenistic History.* Edited by C. H. Gempf. WUNT 49. Tübingen: Mohr, 1989.

Detailed reassessment of the value of Acts' historicity, chronology, and geography from the perspective of a Classicist/New Testament scholar. Concludes that Luke, a companion of Paul, left us with a historically reliable account of early Christianity in harmony with the chronology and geography of Paul's epistles.

368 H. W. Tajra. *The Trial of St. Paul: A Juridical Exegesis of the Second Half of the Acts of the Apostles.* WUNT 2:35. Tübingen: Mohr, 1989.

Argues for the accuracy of Luke's account based upon the juridical details of Paul's legal encounters in the second half of Acts.

369 R. Trigg. "Tales Artfully Spun." Pp. 117–32 in *The Bible as Rhetoric: Studies in Biblical Persuasion and Credibility.* Edited by M. Warner. Warwick Studies in Philosophy and Language. London: Routledge, 1990.

Cautionary essay concerning the removal of Luke-Acts or any of the New Testament writings from the realm of historical truth claims on the basis of modern literary or scientific criteria. The distinction between myth *(muthos)* and claims to truth *(logoi)* are not modern but ancient. "To suggest that an account (or *logos*) can carry a meaning even if it is based on lying or mistaken witness is not in the spirit of the New Testament. . . . Keeping the message of a story while denying its truth is to treat the accounts as *muthoi* and not *logoi*" (p. 132).

370 R. G. Hall. *Revealed Histories: Techniques for Ancient Jewish and Christian Historiography* (esp. pp. 171–208). Journal for the Study of the Pseudepigrapha Supplement Series 6. Sheffield: JSOT Press, 1991.

As with Josephus, we may infer from Luke-Acts the intention to write prophetic history. Both the witnesses in and author of Luke-Acts exhibit the technique of interpretive prophetic history.

371 M. A. Powell. "Reading Acts as History." *Asbury Theological Journal* 46 (1991): 49–62.

Concise history of scholarship which seeks to read Acts as ancient historiography and use it as a source for church history, including how various scholars treat material from Acts which is confirmed by, supplementary to, and in tension with other sources.

372 B. W. Winter and A. D. Clarke (eds.) *The Book of Acts in Its First Century Setting,* Vol. 1: *The Book of Acts in Its Ancient Literary Setting.* Grand Rapids: Eerdmans/Carlisle: Paternoster, 1993.

The first of a projected six-volume series designed to locate Acts as much as possible in its first-century setting. The fourteen essays collected here discuss such "literary" issues as the identification of Acts as an historical monograph (D. W. Palmer), the relationship between Luke and Acts (I. H. Marshall), the question of Acts and the Pauline corpus (B. Winter et al.), the text of Acts (P. Head), and so on.

10.2 Sources and Traditions in Acts

Following the publication of the commentary on Acts by E. Haenchen (#29), many scholars moved away from the source-critical analysis of Acts, due to Haenchen's judgments regarding Luke's literary and theological imagination. It ended a development earlier in this century, when evidence of traditional *accounts* and disparate traditional *materials* were regularly sought. Even those studies failed to attract scholarly consensus, however. This whole debate has now been revisited in the work of C. J.

Hemer (cf. #367, pp. 335–64). See also the ongoing study of traditional materials in the speeches in Acts (§10.3.4).

373 A. von Harnack. *The Acts of the Apostles* (esp. pp. 162–202). Translated by J. R. Wilkinson. London: William & Norgate, 1909.

An early, classical discussion of the sources of Acts, arguing for three sources for the first half of Acts.

374 C. C. Torrey. *The Composition and Date of Acts.* Harvard Theological Studies 1. Cambridge, Mass.: Harvard University Press, 1916.

The classic argument for a continuous, Aramaic source underlying Acts 1–15, in light of which the second half of Acts was written.

375 M. Dibelius. "Style Criticism of the Book of Acts." Pp. 1–25 in *Studies in the Acts of the Apostles.* Edited by H. Greeven. Translated by M. Ling. London: SCM/New York: Charles Scribner's Sons, 1956. Original title: "Stilkritisches zur Apostelgeschichte." Pp. 9–28 in *Aufsätze zur Apostelgeschichte.* FRLANT 60. Göttingen: Vandenhoeck & Ruprecht, 1951. Second edition: 1953.

On the basis of stylistic concerns, an attempt to demarcate generally between tradition and Lukan composition in Acts.

376 J. Dupont. *The Sources of the Acts.* Translated by K. Pond. New York: Herder & Herder, 1964. British edition: *The Sources of Acts: The Present Position.* London: Darton, Longman and Todd, 1964. Original title: *Les Sources du Livre des Actes: État de la Question.* Desclée: de Brouweer, 1960.

Although attempts to locate sources behind Acts have not met with widespread agreement, study has indicated that everywhere Luke has imprinted his traditional materials with his own vocabulary and style.

377 J. Jervell. "The Problem of Traditions in Acts." Pp. 19–39 in *Luke and the People of God: A New Look at Luke-Acts.* Minneapolis: Augsburg, 1972. Original title: "Zur Frage der

Traditionsgrundlage der Apostelgeschichte." *Studia Theologica* 16 (1962): 25–41.

Contra the assumptions of Dibelius and Haenchen, conditions in apostolic times were favorable to the development of traditions about the apostles; such traditions could very well have been used by Luke.

378 M. Wilcox. *The Semitisms of Acts.* Oxford: Clarendon, 1965.

Argues that the evidence does not support Luke's translation of a continuous Aramaic or Hebrew document, though he may have made use of traditional material, particularly in the speeches.

379 G. Lüdemann. *Early Christianity according to the Traditions in Acts: A Commentary.* Translated by J. Bowden. London: SCM/Minneapolis: Fortress, 1989. Original title: *Das frühe Christentum nach den Traditionen der Apostelgeschichte: Ein Kommentar.* Göttingen: Vandenhoeck & Ruprecht, 1987.

A section-by-section commentary on the Acts of the Apostles dividing the material of the text into tradition and redaction; comments on the historicity of the narrated events conclude each section.

380 G. Lüdemann. "Acts of the Apostles as a Historical Source." Pp. 109–25 in *The Social World of Formative Christianity and Judaism: Essays in Tribute to Howard Clark Kee.* Edited by J. Neusner et al. Philadelphia: Fortress, 1988.

Although the chronological framework of Acts is unreliable and must be rejected in favor of a chronology formulated solely on the basis of the Pauline letters, Acts employs traditions that remain an important source, alongside the Pauline materials, for the history of early Christianity.

381 T. C. Smith. "The Sources of Acts." Pp. 55–75 in *With Steadfast Purpose: Essays on Acts in Honor of Henry Jackson Flanders Jr.* Edited by N. H. Keathley. Waco, Tex.: Baylor University Press, 1990.

A discussion of attempts in this century to locate the sources of Acts under the following headings: an Aramaic source for chapters 1–15, sources from places and persons, use of Josephus, the "we" passages, and the speeches in Acts.

10.3 Issues in Lukan Historiography

New Testament scholars typically agree that Luke's status as an historian must be measured not so much against his probable intentions but against his actual performance. On this question, a handful of issues have come into particular focus, and these are discussed in the following sub-sections. (See §5.5 for the recent question of the historical value of Luke's presentation of the "God-fearers.") On another front, because Acts presents in such stark terms the presence of the supernatural, it has proven unacceptable as an historical document to a number of modern New Testament historians who regard its worldview as primitive, its (presumed "seeing-is-believing") spirituality as too superficial. Consequently, the presence of the supernatural has also come under scrutiny in the discussion of the historical value of Acts (on the demonic, see above, §5.2).

10.3.1 The Census in Luke 2 as an Historical Problem

The problems of the census of Luke 2 have continued to be discussed throughout this century. The arguments, harmonizations, and reconstructions are legion. The basic problems addressed in these studies include the problem of a *Roman* census in Herod's *Jewish* kingdom during his reign; the lack of evidence for a census of the entire empire; the apparent want of any requirement for Joseph to return to Bethlehem; and Josephus' conflicting account of the census in 6–7 C.E. as the first of this nature.

382 W. M. Ramsay. "Luke's Narrative of the Birth of Jesus." *The Expositor* 8/14 (1912): 385–407, 481–507.

> Proposes the co-governorship of Quirinius and Saturninus, and defends the possibility of the census' requirement of returning to one's birthplace.

383 W. M. Ramsay. *The Bearing of Recent Discovery on the Trustworthiness of the New Testament*, pp. 238–300. James Sprunt Lectures. Aberdeen: Aberdeen University Press,

1913. Reprinted London: Hodder & Stoughton. Fourth edition: 1920.

Suggests Quirinius was co-governor with one of the already existing, known governors, possibly Sentius Saturninus.

384 T. Corbishley. "A Note on the Date of the Syrian Governorship of M. Titius." *Journal of Roman Studies* 24 (1933): 43–49.

Contra Josephus, dates the governorship of M. Titius prior to 12 B.C.E., thereby leaving enough time for Quirinius prior to Saturninus' legateship.

385 L. R. Taylor. "Quirinius and the Census of Syria." *American Journal of Philology* 54 (1933): 120–33.

Though wrong in naming Quirinius governor of Syria before the death of Herod, "Luke may be right in saying that a census of Judea took place in the days of Herod for which everyone was commanded to return to his own city. It is perhaps not impossible that this census was part of an enrollment of all the populations of the Roman world" (p. 133).

386 T. Corbishley. "Quirinius and the Census: A Re-study of the Evidence." *Klio* 29 (1936): 81–93.

Shows high regard for the trustworthiness of Luke's account, both that Quirinius was governor of Syria during the years 11–8 B.C.E., and for the possibility of a universal enrollment of Romans and non-Romans: "the evidence pointing to a fairly universal censorial activity in different parts of the Empire in the years between 11 and 8 B.C., without being conclusive proof of the proclamation of a dogma about this time, is so abundant that St. Luke's statement is only another example of the value of his evidence for the details of Imperial administration" (p. 90).

387 A. N. Sherwin-White. "Quirinius: A Note." Pp. 162–71 in *Roman Society and Roman Law in the New Testament.* Oxford: Oxford University, 1963. Reprinted Grand Rapids: Baker, 1978.

Contends for the accuracy of Luke's account based on the uncertainty concerning who was legate in Syria in the last years of Herod's reign, on Quirinius' prominence in the area during the period prior to Jesus' birth, and on Augustus' manner of ordering particular actions couched within explanations which included the entire empire.

388 J. Finegan. *Handbook of Biblical Chronology,* pp. 234–38. Princeton: Princeton University Press, 1964.

Argues for the possibility of Quirinius' involvement, in some form or fashion, in the census project with Saturninus. Moreover, Herod's demotion from "friend" to "subject" of Rome during this time, as well as Quirinius' census of the autonomous city-state of Apamea on the Orontes in Syria lends further plausibility.

389 G. M. Lee. "The Census in Luke." *Church Quarterly Review* 167 (1966): 431–36.

A tentative reconstruction of events surrounding Jesus' birth which removes historical difficulties concerning the census yet does not contradict Luke's explicit statements.

390 G. Ogg. "The Quirinius Question Today." *ExpTim* 79 (1967–68): 231–36.

Survey of proposed solutions to the problematic chronology of Luke 2:2, concluding that the current tendency is to assume that Luke has incorrectly dated Jesus' birth as occurring in 6–7 C.E.

391 A. J. B. Higgins. "Sidelights on Christian Beginnings in the Greco-Roman World." *Evangelical Quarterly* 41 (1969): 197–206.

Proposes a chronologically less problematic translation of Luke 2:2 as, "This census took place before Quirinius was governor of Syria."

392 H. R. Moehring. "The Census in Luke as an Apologetic Device." Pp. 144–60 in *Studies in New Testament and Related Literature: Essays in Honor of Allen P. Wikgren.* Edited by D. E. Aune. NovTSup 33. Leiden: Brill, 1972.

Luke's statement concerning the census under Quirinius is historically inaccurate, yet serves the apologetic function of connecting the double origins of both Jesus and Christianity in Judaism and the Roman empire. This episode contributes to Luke's overarching portrayal of Christians as the true Jews, even in the Roman legal sense, who have never rebelled against Rome.

393 D. J. Hayles. "The Roman Census and Jesus' Birth. Was Luke Correct? Part I: The Roman Census System." *Buried History* 9 (1973): 113–32.

Sketches a general picture of the administration of the census under Augustus and the twelve-year census cycle in Syria. Based on the accounts of Josephus in *Antiquities* 18.1 and Acts 5:37 of a census in 6–7 C.E., the previous census would have been in 6–5 B.C.E. Moreover, the worldwide census may refer to a continuing enrollment under Augustus, though Luke limits the extent of the census to Syria and Palestine. Luke's account of a census at the time of the birth of Jesus fits well within this outline.

394 E. M. Schürer, *The History of the Jewish People in the Age of Jesus Christ (175 B.C.–A.D. 135)* I, pp. 399–427. Leipzig: J. C. Hinrichs, 1886. Reprinted, revised, and edited by G. Vermes and F. Miller. Edinburgh: T. & T. Clark, 1973.

After giving a general overview of the Roman system of taxation during the imperial period, and enumerating the problems raised by Luke's account, concludes that Luke combines various provincial censuses into one imperial census and dated the Judaean census 10–12 years early.

395 P. W. Barnett. "ἀπογραφή and ἀπογράφεσθαι." *ExpTim* 85 (1973–74): 377–80.

Raises the possibility that Luke 2:1–5 may refer to an oath of allegiance rather than the problematic tax enrollment of 6–7 C.E.

396 D. J. Hayles. "The Roman Census and Jesus' Birth. Was Luke Correct? Part II: Quirinius' Career and a Census in Herod's Day." *Buried History* 10 (1974): 16–31.

Because of his victorious crusade against the Homonadenses in the region, and Tiberius' early retirement to Rhodes in 6 C.E., Quirinius may have provided administrative continuity between the legates of Saturninus and Varus, while Herod was yet king, in accord with Luke's account.

397 E. M. Smallwood. *The Jews under Roman Rule: From Pompey to Diocletian*, pp. 568–71. Studies in Judaism in Late Antiquity 20. Leiden: Brill, 1976.

Concise overview of the problems and arguments posited, concluding that Luke erroneously attached the name Quirinius, who was responsible for a later census, to an earlier census which coincided with Jesus' birth.

398 R. E. Brown. "The Census under Quirinius." Pp. 547–56 in *The Birth of the Messiah*. Garden City, N.Y.: Doubleday, 1977.

Excellent overview of the text's difficulties, with a thorough assessment of scholarship addressing the issue, emphasizing Luke's theological purposes.

399 J. Thorley. "The Nativity Census: What Does Luke Actually Say?" *Greece and Rome* 26 (1979): 81–84.

Proposes that Luke 2:1–2 indicates that, over a period of time and in separate regions, Augustus' decree extended the census to the entire Roman world; also that the census was the first carried out in Judea while Quirinius was governor in Syria, separate from the second census of 6 C.E.

400 R. Smith. "Caesar's Decree (Luke 1:1–2): Puzzle or Key?" *CTM* 7 (1980): 343–51.

Though the chronological and historical problems of Luke 2:1–2 have not been solved, Joseph's portrayal as an obedient, law abiding citizen can be understood within Luke's political apologetic toward Rome.

401 W. Brindle. "The Census and Quirinius—Luke 2:2." *Journal of the Evangelical Theological Society* 27 (1984): 43–52.

Considers when Quirinius was governor of Syria and when exactly the census took place, asserting that the census of Luke 2:2 should be understood as occurring in the days of Herod the Great, before the more well known one taken by Quirinius.

402 T. P. Wiseman. "There went out a decree from Caesar Augustus. . . ." *NTS* 33 (1987): 479–80.

Proposes, in light of Augustus' inheritance tax introduced in 6 C.E., that Quirinius carried out the necessary census for this tax at the same time as his provincial census. Hence, Luke's account may be historical though lacking precise accuracy.

403 G. D. Kilpatrick. "Luke 2,4–5 and Leviticus 25,10." *Zeitschrift für die neutestamentliche Wissenschaft* 80 (1989): 263–65.

Suggests that the echo of the Jubilee text in Leviticus motivated Luke to develop his account of the census to bring Joseph and Mary from Nazareth to Bethlehem.

404 C. J. Humphrey. "The Star of Bethlehem, a Comet in 5 B.C. and the Date of Christ's Birth." *TynB* 43 (1992): 31–56.

On the basis of astronomical data, posits Jesus' birth in 5 B.C.E., in harmony with Josephus' account of a census enrollment at this time.

10.3.2 Miracles and the Supernatural in Luke-Acts

For persons committed to the "modern scientific worldview," the miracles of Jesus already constitute a problem. But this dilemma is exacerbated all the more by the reports of spectacular healing and divine intervention in Acts. It is for this reason that the presence of miracles and the supernatural have constituted an obstacle to the believability of Acts as an historical document (cf. #367, pp. 428–43). Earlier investigations of these phenomena moved forward on the basis of Newtonian science—that is, on the basis of a mechanics that urged that we can understand cause-and-effect in a predictable way. In such a world, miracles are not possible, for the "miraculous" *effect* of scientific necessity must have a natural *cause* (Hume). Contemporary studies of these phenomena will have to take account of the reality that, at the close of the twentieth century, there is no agreed upon, common, modern, scientific view of the world. And the miraculous phenomena noted in the Gospels and Acts—previously understood as expressions of deception, mental pathology, superstition, fantasy, and a pre-scientific worldview—have re-entered (post)modern discourse as exemplars of the mysterious in our world, of a reality larger than what can (yet) be measured by physical sensors. In the interim, however, the miracles in Acts are being scrutinized not so much for their historicity as for the social and narratological purpose they serve for Luke.

405 J. A. Hardon. "Miracle Narratives in the Acts of the Apostles." *CBQ* 16 (1954): 303–18.

  The miracles reported in Acts help to explain the rise of the early church and demonstrate the continued presence of Jesus by means of the Spirit in its ministry.

406 G. W. H. Lampe. "Miracles in the Acts of the Apostles." Pp. 163–78 in *Miracles: Cambridge Studies in Their Philosophy and History*. Edited by C. F. D. Moule. London: A. R. Mowbray, 1965.

  In Acts, Luke is not working with a "miracle-apologetic," as though the presence of miracles proves the veracity of Christian doctrine, but rather to show how the ministry of Jesus extends through the working of the Holy Spirit, from Galilee in the Third Gospel, through the apostles to Rome in Acts.

407 P. J. Achtemeier. "The Lucan Perspective on the Miracles of Jesus: A Preliminary Sketch." *JBL* 94 (1975): 547–62. Reprinted in *Perspectives on Luke-Acts*, pp. 152–67. Edited by C. H. Talbert. Danville, Va.: Association of Baptist Professors of Religion/Edinburgh: T. & T. Clark, 1978.

  A redaction-critical study of the Lukan perspective on Jesus' miracles, arguing that Luke uses miracles less critically than the other Evangelists, in order to serve as the basis for faith in Jesus; he has done so, however, without subordinating his presentation of Jesus to a magical worldview.

408 F. Neirynck. "The Miracle Stories in the Acts of the Apostles: An Introduction." *Ephemerides Theologicae Lovanienses* 55 (1979): 169–213. Reprinted: Pp. 169–213 in *Les Actes des Apôtres: Traditions, Rédaction, Théologie*. Edited by J. Kremer. BETL 48. Leuven: Leuven University, 1979; also in Neirynck's *Evangelica: Gospel Studies—Études D'Évangile. Collected Essays*, pp. 835–79. Edited by F. van Segbroeck. BETL 60. Leuven: Leuven University Press, 1982.

  A major description of the miracle stories in Acts, with sections devoted to Peter-Paul and Jesus-Peter/Paul parallels; source criticism; form criticism; Lukan redaction; and the special problem of Acts 3:16.

409 D. E. Aune. "Magic in Early Christianity." *ANRW* 2.23.2:1507–57 (1980).

A critical survey of the relationship of ancient magic to early Christianity attempting to provide a "comprehensive and consistent theoretical framework" and "highlight the lacunae" in this area of scholarship (p. 1050).

410 J. S. Hanson. "Dreams and Visions in the Graeco-Roman World and Early Christianity." *ANRW* 2.23.2:1395–427 (1980).

Delineates the literary form and function of the dream-vision report in Greco-Roman literature and illustrates the process of its elaboration in early Christian literature.

411 A. B. Kolenkow. "Relationships between Miracle and Prophecy in the Greco-Roman World and Early Christianity." *ANRW* 2.23.2:1470–506 (1980).

Surveys the various opinions that existed between the relationship and interaction of miracle and prophecy in the Greco-Roman world and early Christian communities.

412 H. C. Kee. *Miracle in the Early Christian World: A Study in Sociohistorical Method*, pp. 190–220. New Haven: Yale University Press, 1983.

A socio-cultural examination; Kee concludes, "For Luke miracle functions, not only to heighten the drama of the narrative, but also to show that at every significant point in the transitions from its Jewish origins in Jerusalem to its Gentile outreaching to Rome itself, the hand of God is evidence in the form of public miraculous confirmation" (p. 220).

413 E. M. Yamauchi. "Magic in the Biblical World." *TynB* 34 (1983): 169–200.

Situates encounters like those in Acts 8:9–24; 13:6–12; 19:17–20 within the context of a world steeped with occult beliefs and practices.

414 D. Hamm. "Acts 3:12–26: Peter's Speech and the Healing of the Man Born Lame." *PRS* 11 (1984): 199–217.

The healing of the man born lame (Acts 3:1–10) demonstrates that Jesus has been raised to reign as the Davidic
Messiah, as well as to continue his mission as the
prophet-like-Moses who is now active via his followers.

415 J. B. Green. "Jesus and a Daughter of Abraham (Luke 13:10–
17): Test Case for a Lucan Perspective on Jesus' Miracles."
CBQ 51 (1989): 643–54.
Jesus' healing ministry is set within the context of an eschatological battle and points to the realization of Jesus'
program of ministry as announced in the synagogue at
Nazareth (Luke 4:18–19).

416 J. J. Pilch. "Sickness and Healing in Luke-Acts." *The Bible
Today* 27 (1989): 21–28.
A helpful introduction to the study of sickness and heal-
ing in Luke-Acts from a social-scientific perspective.

10.3.3 The Apostolic Council

Luke's chronology of the Jerusalem council and Paul's visits to
Jerusalem in Acts 9, 11, and 15 are problematic in light of Paul's
account in Galatians 1–2. The primary issue revolves around the
discrepancies between Acts 15 and Galatians 2, both of which
purport to deal with the Jew-Gentile problem in early Christianity. Related problems include: Should Luke be considered a major
rival source to Paul? Was Luke's account in Acts 15 (or Acts 9 or
11) largely shaped or created by Luke's hand? If so, what historical
events are being shaped or synthesized by Luke, and to what end?
Finally, should the assumed date of Galatians be reassessed in
light of Acts?

417 K. Lake. "The Apostolic Council of Jerusalem." Pp. 195–212
in *The Beginnings of Christianity*, Part One: *The Acts of the
Apostles*, Vol. 5: *Additional Notes to the Commentary*. Edited by F. J. Foakes-Jackson and K. Lake. London: Macmillan, 1922–1933. Reprinted Grand Rapids: Baker, 1979.
Overview of the major problems and positions, concluding that the conference in Jerusalem described in Galatians 2 was concerned with circumcision and the applica-
bility of the law to Gentile Christians. To this council
Luke has mistakenly connected a decree which estab-

lished rules of conduct for social intercourse between Jewish and Gentile Christians.

418 J. Knox. "The Evidence of Acts." Pp. 43–52 in *Chapters in a Life of Paul.* New York: Abingdon, 1950. Reprinted Macon, Ga.: Mercer University Press, 1987.

Concludes that "there can be little doubt that the meeting in Jerusalem that Luke represents as an impressive apostolic council in Acts 15:1–29 is the same meeting that Paul has more accurately described in Galatians 2:1–10" (p. 44).

419 M. Dibelius. "The Apostolic Council." Pp. 93–101 in *Studies in the Acts of the Apostles.* Edited by H. Greeven. Translated by M. Ling. London: SCM/New York: Charles Scribner's Sons, 1956. Original title: "Das Apostelkonzil." Pp. 84–90 in *Aufsätze zur Apostelgeschichte.* FRLANT 60. Göttingen: Vandenhoeck & Ruprecht, 1951. Second edition: 1953.

Acts 15 is not "a serious rival source" to the report in Galatians 2, but is told to further Luke's thesis that God had "revealed his will that the gospel should be freely carried to the Gentiles" (pp. 101, 99).

420 P. Parker. "Once More, Acts and Galatians." *JBL* (1967): 175–82.

Attempts to reconcile major discrepancies between Acts 15 and Galatians 2 for a harmonious chronology, concluding that only Paul's visit to Jerusalem in Acts 9 is a Lukan creation composed from later visits.

421 C. H. Talbert. "Again: Paul's Visits to Jerusalem." *NovT* 9 (1967): 26–40.

Proposes that Paul's letter to the Galatians originated soon after the Jerusalem council. Since Paul's response to the Galatians echoes the visit of Acts 15 then Galatians 1:18ff. corresponds to Acts 9, and Galatians 2:1ff. corresponds to Acts 11–12.

422 G. Zuntz. "An Analysis of the Report about the 'Apostolic Council.'" Pp. 216–49 in *Opuscula Selecta.* Manchester: Manchester University Press, 1972.

Employs text-critical, structural, and stylistic criteria to discern the historical substratum of the account, concluding that Luke has combined an anti-Pauline account of the council with a second decree from James concerning the observance of certain food-laws to form "an edifying story stressing the essential and exemplary unity of the Primitive church" (p. 249).

423 R. H. Stein. "The Relationship of Galatians 2:1–10 and Acts 15:1–35: Two Neglected Arguments." *Journal of the Evangelical Theological Society* 17 (1974): 239–42.

A survey of arguments and positions in this debate, concluding that Galatians 2:1–10 and Acts 15:1–35 refer to the same event and best explain Paul's role in it.

424 D. R. Catchpole. "Paul, James and the Apostolic Decree." *NTS* 23 (1976–77): 428–44.

Concludes that the apostolic decree stems from pre-Lukan tradition, embraces Mosaic law for Gentiles among Jews, and, hence, was rejected by Paul, leading to the isolation of Paul and his mission. The decree did not stem from the apostolic conference in Galatians 2, rather, the problems at Antioch in Galatians 2:11–14 arose from its implementation.

425 C. J. Hemer. "Observations on Pauline Chronology." Pp. 3–18 in *Pauline Studies: Essays Presented to Professor F. F. Bruce on His 70th Birthday.* Edited by D. A. Hagner and M. J. Harris. Grand Rapids: Eerdmans, 1980.

A reexamination of the alleged fixed points of dating Pauline chronology, leading to a tentative framework for Paul's ministry able to accommodate "the view which dated Galatians early, before the Council of Jerusalem . . . this permits a straightforward identification of the Jerusalem visits in Acts with those in Galatians" (p. 12).

426 P. J. Achtemeier. "An Elusive Unity: Paul, Acts, and the Early Church." *CBQ* 48 (1986): 1–26.

Concise treatment of themes developed in *Quest* (#427), understanding the apostolic decree as the cause of conflict in Galatians 2 rather than its outcome; hence, the unity portrayed stems from Luke's hand and Paul became increasingly isolated from Jerusalem.

427 P. J. Achtemeier. *The Quest for Unity in the New Testament.* Philadelphia: Fortress, 1987.

Reconstructs the events underlying Acts and Galatians and reflects on their implications concerning church unity from the understanding that the main dispute occurred after and as a result of the apostolic council rather than prior to, then resolved by, that council.

428 C. J. Hemer. *The Book of Acts in the Setting of Hellenistic History,* pp. 244–76. Edited by C. H. Gempf. WUNT 49. Tübingen: Mohr, 1989.

Hypothesizes that Galatians was the earliest of Paul's epistles; and that Acts 9 corresponds to Galatians 1, Acts 11 to Galatians 2. The council of Acts 15 had not taken place at the time of the writing of Galatians.

10.3.4 The Speeches in Acts

How far Luke was able to draw on traditional material in writing the speeches in Acts, and how far those speeches derive from Lukan creativity, has been a hotly debated question since the middle of this century (cf. #367, pp. 415–27). Study along this line continues, though it is now being supplemented by other concerns—especially those related to how these speeches function as integral to the Acts narrative as it is read from beginning to end, and as it builds on the story of God's redemptive plan in the Old Testament and in the Gospel of Luke. (See also the relevant essays in #372.)

429 C. H. Dodd. *The Apostolic Preaching and Its Developments: With an Appendix on Eschatology and History.* London: Hodder & Stoughton, 1936. Reprinted Grand Rapids: Baker, 1980.

Argues for a standard, traditional outline of early Christian preaching represented in the missionary speeches of Acts.

430 F. F. Bruce. *The Speeches in the Acts of the Apostles.* London: Tyndale, 1942.

Although the speeches in Acts are not verbatim reports, they are "faithful epitomes, giving the gist of the arguments used" (p. 27).

431 M. Dibelius. "Paul on the Areopagus." Pp. 26–77 in *Studies in the Acts of the Apostles.* Edited by H. Greeven. Translated by M. Ling. London: SCM/New York: Charles Scribner's Sons, 1956. Original title: "Paulus auf dem Areopag." Pp. 29–70 in *Aufsätze zur Apostelgeschichte.* FRLANT 60. Göttingen: Vandenhoeck & Ruprecht, 1951. Second edition: 1953.

"Paul on the Areopagus" is not an historical but a symbolic encounter between Christian theology and Greek culture.

432 M. Dibelius. "The Speeches in Acts and Ancient Historiography." Pp. 138–85 in *Studies in the Acts of the Apostles.* Edited by H. Greeven. Translated by M. Ling. London: SCM/New York: Charles Scribner's Sons, 1956. Original title: "Die Reden der Apostelgeschichte und die antike Geschichtsschreibung." Pp. 120–62 in *Aufsätze zur Apostelgeschichte.* FRLANT 60. Göttingen: Vandenhoeck & Ruprecht, 1951. Second edition: 1953.

The speeches in Acts come from the hand of Luke, who followed the ancient historians in composing speeches, while putting this practice to a new use in communicating the ways of God.

433 B. Gärtner. *The Areopagus and Natural Revelation.* Lund: C. W. K. Gleerup, 1955.

Argues that nothing in Paul's address to the Athenians in Acts 17 clashes with what is otherwise known of Pauline theology from his letters; for this speech, Luke is building on a tradition from Paul's visit to Athens.

434 E. Schweizer. "Concerning the Speeches in Acts." Pp. 208–16 in *Studies in Luke-Acts* (P. Schubert Festschrift). Edited by L. E. Keck and J. L. Martyn. Nashville: Abingdon, 1966. Original title: "Zu den Reden der Apostelgeschichte." *Theologische Zeitschrift* 13 (1957): 1–11. Reprinted in Schweizer's *Neotestamentica: Deutsche und Englische Aufsätze 1951–*

1963—German and English Essays 1951–1963, pp. 418–298.
Zürich/Stüttgart: Zwingli, 1963.

Building on ##431, 432 analyzes the content of the missionary speeches delivered to Jew and Gentile audiences and concludes that they are Lukan in composition, though he occasionally has taken up traditional material.

435 H. Conzelmann. "The Address of Paul on the Areopagus." Pp. 217–30 in *Studies in Luke-Acts* (P. Schubert Festschrift). Edited by L. E. Keck and J. L. Martyn. Nashville: Abingdon, 1966. Original title: "Die Rede des Paulus auf dem Areopag." *Gymnasium Helveticum* 12 (1958): 18–32.

Paul's speech at Athens is not drawn from an historical occasion but neither is it presented as a "model sermon"; after all, this "unique" attempt to draw on popular religion in order to engage the Athenian philosophers was unsuccessful.

436 J. T. Townsend. "The Speeches in Acts." *Anglican Theological Review* 42 (1960): 150–59.

The speeches of Acts reflect only one point of view and, far from being context-specific, are interdependent; they are Lukan in origin.

437 U. Wilckens. *Die Missionsreden der Apostelgeschichte: Form- und traditionsgeschichtliche Untersuchungen*. Wissenschaftliche Monographien zum Alten und Neuen Testament 5. Neukirchen-Vluyn: Neukirchener, 1961. Second edition: 1963. Third edition: 1974.

The most comprehensive discussion of the speeches in Acts available today; finds in the missionary speeches of Acts a common plan that is not primitive but Lukan.

438 J. W. Bowker. "Speeches in Acts: A Study in Proem and Yelammedenu Form." *NTS* 14 (1967–68): 96–111.

An examination of selected ingredients of the speech material in Acts demonstrates its affinity with the style of argumentation of homilies in synagogues.

439 P. Schubert. "The Final Cycle of Speeches in the Book of Acts." *JBL* 87 (1968): 1–16.

Luke has departed from the Thucydidean model by incorporating his speech material fully into the narrative as a whole; the speeches and their contexts account for almost three-quarters of the narrative of Acts, underscoring the character of Acts as the story of the proclamation of the word of God.

440 E. E. Ellis. "Midrashic Features in the Speeches of Acts." Pp. 303–12 in *Mélanges Bibliques en hommage au R. P. Béda Rigaux*. Edited by A. Descamps and A. de Halleux. Gembloux: J. Duculot, 1970.

Midrashic features in the speeches of Acts 2 and 13 support the view that Luke is drawing on traditional material in constructing these addresses.

441 C. F. Evans. "'Speeches' in Acts." Pp. 287–302 in *Mélanges Bibliques en hommage au R. P. Béda Rigaux*. Edited by A. Descamps and A. de Halleux. Gembloux: J. Duculot, 1970.

The addresses in Acts fall into the category of "speeches," in the sense of Hellenistic history, rather than of "sermons"; this suggests that Luke's audience could well have been the world outside the church to an extent greater than any other New Testament writing.

442 R. F. Zehnle. *Peter's Pentecost Discourse: Tradition and Lukan Reinterpretation in Peter's Speeches in Acts 2 and 3*. Society of Biblical Literature Monograph Series 15. Nashville/New York: Abingdon, 1971.

The Pentecost address in Acts 2 is a Lukan composition, though the speech of Peter in Acts 3 shows signs of having been drawn from primitive material.

443 F. F. Bruce. "The Speeches in Acts—Thirty Years Later." Pp. 53–68 in *Reconciliation and Hope: New Testament Essays on Atonement and Eschatology Presented to L. L. Morris on His 60th Birthday*. Edited by R. Banks. Grand Rapids: Eerdmans, 1974.

A follow-up to #430, reviewing major studies of the speeches in Acts in the interim and discussing selected theological material from the speeches by way of postulating their suitability to the speakers to whom they are attributed.

444 W. W. Gasque. "The Speeches of Acts: Dibelius Reconsidered." Pp. 232–51 in *New Dimensions in New Testament Study.* Edited by R. N. Longenecker and M. C. Tenney. Grand Rapids: Zondervan, 1974.

Although Dibelius moved the study of Acts in a helpful direction with his emphasis on Luke as an author with literary ambition, Gasque insists that Dibelius' judgment that the speeches of Acts are Lukan compositions (apart from tradition) flies in the face of the available evidence.

445 M. Wilcox. "A Foreword to the Study of the Speeches in Acts." Pp. 206–25 in *Christianity, Judaism and Other Greco-Roman Cults: Studies for Morton Smith at Sixty,* Part One: *New Testament.* Edited by J. Neusner. Studies in Judaism in Late Antiquity 12. Leiden: Brill, 1975.

Presents a positive answer to the question of locating historical and/or traditional material in the speeches in Acts, then presents four criteria for discerning pre-Lukan tradition: language and style (esp. Semitisms), appropriateness to a Jewish-Christian setting, objective comparison with New Testament parallels outside Acts, and apparent inconsistencies within a speech and its context.

446 J. Kilgallen. *The Stephen Speech: A Literary and Redactional Study of Acts 7,2–53.* Analecta Biblica 67. Rome: Pontifical Biblical Institute Press, 1976.

Although Luke may have had use of traditional material in his composition of the Stephen speech, as it now stands in his narrative it is thoroughly Lukan; herein it is argued that "Jewish rejection of faith in the Savior Christ cannot but result in a worship that is no longer of value to God" (p. 120).

447 C. K. Barrett. "Paul's Address to the Ephesian Elders." Pp. 107–21 in *God's Christ and His People: Studies in Honour of Nils Alstrup Dahl.* Edited by J. Jervell and W. A. Meeks. Oslo: Universitetsforlaget, 1977.

Luke used general Pauline tradition in composing this speech and helped to ensure by this speech the continuation of the apostolic mission in the spirit of Paul.

448 B. E. Shields. "The Areopagus Sermon and Romans 1:18ff: A Study in Creation Theology." *Restoration Quarterly* 20 (1977): 23–40.

Romans 1–2 and the address of Paul in Acts 17 are complementary rather than contradictory, demonstrating that the early church was willing to borrow from contemporary philosophy in order to proclaim God's self-revelation.

449 M. B. Bland. "The Speeches in Acts." *Evangelical Quarterly* 50 (1978): 147–55.

Reviews a variety of perspectives on the historicity of the speeches in Acts, concluding that "the intention behind each record is an accuracy of reporting" (p. 155).

450 M. M. Scharlemann. "Acts 7:2–53. Stephen's Speech: A Lucan Creation?" *Concordia Journal* 4 (1978): 52–57.

"[T]he author of Luke-Acts gives us in substance, and frequently in the very phrases of Stephen, the message of one who realized that the temple in Jerusalem stood as an obstacle in the way of bringing the 'good news' to Samaria" (p. 57).

451 F. Veltman. "The Defense Speeches of Paul in Acts." Pp. 243–56 in *Perspectives on Luke-Acts.* Edited by C. H. Talbert. Danville, Va.: Association of Baptist Professors of Religion/Edinburgh: T. & T. Clark, 1978.

Argues that the defense speeches of Paul in Acts follow the general pattern of defense speeches in ancient literature.

452 J. Lambrecht. "Paul's Farewell Address on Miletus (Acts 20,17–38)." Pp. 307–37 in *Les Actes des Apôtres: Traditions, Rédaction, Théologie.* Edited by J. Kremer. BETL 48. Leuven: Leuven University Press, 1979.

Luke has composed this address and located it here in the overall narrative for pastoral purposes—especially to address "post-apostolic difficulties" in the church of his day, including the need to continue assistance to the poor.

453 C. H. H. Scobie. "The Use of Source Material in the Speeches of Acts III and IV." *NTS* 25 (1979): 399–421.

Luke made use of "an early Christian tract" in his composition of the Petrine speech in Acts 3:12–26 and of the Stephen speech in Acts 7:2–53.

454 F. G. Downing. "Ethical Paganism and the Speeches in Acts." *NTS* 27 (1981): 544–63.

Theorizes that "Luke is portraying the teachings of the Christians as a creditable variant of the kind of ethical providential monotheism that educated pagans might be expected to attend to respectfully" (p. 544).

455 C. A. Evans. "The Prophetic Setting of the Pentecost Sermon." *Zeitschrift für die neutestamentliche Wissenschaft* 74 (1983): 148–50.

In Acts 2 (and perhaps elsewhere), Luke has not so much used his literary imagination but the Old Testament prophetic tradition so as to develop and order his narrative.

456 J. Neyrey. "The Forensic Defense Speech and Paul's Trial Speeches in Acts 22–26: Form and Function." Pp. 210–24 in *Luke-Acts: New Perspectives from the Society of Biblical Literature Seminar.* Edited by C. H. Talbert. New York: Crossroad, 1984.

Argues that the trial speeches in Acts follow the models of the forensic defense speech presented in the rhetorical handbooks.

457 R. J. Dillon. "The Prophecy of Christ and His Witnesses according to the Discourses of Acts." *NTS* 32 (1986): 544–56.

Readings of Acts 2:16–21; 3:22–26 highlight the importance of *prophecy* as a category of Luke's christology and as a perceptible point of contact between his narrative and his sources, and suggest the prominence in Luke-Acts of continuity between Jesus and the church.

458 G. H. R. Horsley. "Speeches and Dialogue in Acts." *NTS* 32 (1986): 609–14.

Queries how the speech material functions within the narrative of Acts, relative to other ancient narratives; draws special attention to the number of speeches that are interrupted by characters within the account or by the narrator, and to the relatively heavy and diverse use of direct discourse in Acts.

459 C. J. Hemer. "The Speeches of Acts: 1. The Ephesian Elders at Miletus." *TynB* 40 (1989): 77–85.

Although Luke's editorial hand is not absent from this speech, Hemer argues that it contains "real Paulinisms."

460 C. J. Hemer. "The Speeches of Acts: 2. The Areopagus Address." *TynB* 40 (1989): 239–59.

Argues that the Paul of the epistles and the Paul of this address are the same Paul.

461 D. L. Balch. "The Areopagus Speech: An Appeal to the Stoic Historian Posidonius against Later Stoics and the Epicureans." Pp. 52–79 in *Greeks, Romans, and Christians: Essays in Honor of Abraham J. Malherbe.* Edited by D. L. Balch et al. Minneapolis: Fortress, 1990.

A comparison of the Areopagus speech and Posidonius is undertaken in order to suggest that "Luke-Acts guards the legitimate philosophical tradition against the Athenians who delight in novelties" (p. 79).

462 J. H. Neyrey. "Acts 17, Epicureans, and Theodicy: A Study in Stereotypes." Pp. 118–34 in *Greeks, Romans, and Christians: Essays in Honor of Abraham J. Malherbe.* Edited by D. L. Balch et al. Minneapolis: Fortress, 1990.

The position taken by Luke's Paul in the Areopagus address on two primary issues, providence and theodicy, is one that will be embraced by all reasonable people; a similar argument is presented in Acts 23–24, with the consequence that we understand Luke to be presenting the Christian movement so as to find common ground with those guardians of basic tradition, Hellenistic Stoics and Jewish Pharisees.

463 S. E. Porter. "Thucydides 1.22.1 and Speeches in Acts: Is There a Thucydidean View?" *NovT* 32 (1990): 121–42.

Demonstrates the need for scholars who appeal to Thucidydes' acknowledged procedure in writing speeches to take more seriously the ambiguities of his claim, and to consider his actual practice of speech-writing and not only his problematic programmatic statement.

464 R. B. Sloan. "'Signs and Wonders': A Rhetorical Clue to the Pentecost Discourse." Pp. 145–62 in *With Steadfast Pur-*

pose: Essays on Acts in Honor of Henry Jackson Flanders Jr.
Edited by N. H. Keathley. Waco, Tex.: Baylor University
Press, 1990.

The missiological purpose of the Pentecost address is realized via arguing in the salvation-historical pattern of
the traditional kerygma, the use of a narrative framework
for communicating the kerygma, and the narrative use of
Scripture for explicating the mighty acts of God done in
Jesus.

465 R. C. Tannehill. "The Functions of Peter's Mission Speeches
in the Narrative of Acts." *NTS* 37 (1991): 400–414.

A narrative analysis shows that, although Peter's speeches
in Acts contain common elements and follow a similar
pattern (see #429), the setting of each speech and the way
those elements are deployed portend the importance of
studying each speech as an action in the unfolding narrative.

466 B. Winter. "The Importance of the *Captatio Benevolentiae*
in the Speeches of Tertullus and Paul in Acts 24:1–21." *JTS*
42 (1991): 505–31.

A form-critical analysis of the opening to the legal addresses of Tertullus and Paul in Acts 24 aimed at clarify-
ing their function and undermining attempts to dismiss
easily their historicity.

467 C. Gempf. "Athens, Paul at." Pp. 51–54 in *Dictionary of
Paul and His Letters.* Edited by R. P. Martin et al. Downers
Grove, Ill.: InterVarsity/Leicester: Inter-Varsity, 1993.

Paul's speech to the Athenians in Acts 17 is (1) "a devas-
tating attack on both the Athenians and their religion"
(p. 52) and (2) in harmony with what we know of Paul
from his letters.

10.3.5 The Paulinism of Acts

P. Vielhauer's ground-breaking essay "On the 'Paulinism' of
Acts" concludes, "the author of Acts is in his Christology pre-
Pauline, in his natural theology, concept of the law, and eschatology, post-Pauline" (#468, p. 17). Such an assessment calls into
question many previous assumptions concerning Luke—especially his presumed personal knowledge of Paul, and/or his let-

ters. Can the Paul of his New Testament letters be reconciled with the Paul of Acts? Defenders of Luke's accuracy in his portrayal of Paul seek to underscore internal harmonization or outside corroboration for Acts' historical accuracy or validity as a supplemental source for an understanding of Paul. Other studies seek to disclose motivating historical situations or overriding literary concerns which shaped Luke's account. (Since the question of Luke's possible friendship with Paul is tied together with the nature of the "we-passages" in Acts, see also §10.3.6. On Paul's speeches in Acts, see §10.3.4. See also the relevant essays in #372.)

468 P. Vielhauer. "On the 'Paulinism' of Acts." Translated by W. C. Robinson Jr. and V. P. Furnish. *Perkins School of Theology Journal* 17 (1963): 5–17. Reprinted in *Studies in Luke-Acts* (P. Schubert Festschrift), pp. 33–50. Edited by L. E. Keck and J. L. Martyn. Nashville: Abingdon, 1966. Abridged in *The Writings of St. Paul*, pp. 166–75. Edited by W. A. Meeks. New York: Norton, 1972. Original title: "Zum 'Paulinismus' der Apostelgeschichte." *Evangelische Theologie* 10 (1950–51): 1–15.

   Seminal essay distinguishing the theology of Paul in Acts from Paul of the epistles in the areas of natural theology, the law, christology, eschatology, and ecclesiology. Raises significant questions regarding Luke's temporal and theological distance from Paul.

469 M. Dibelius. "Paul in Athens." Pp. 78–83 in *Studies in the Acts of the Apostles*. Edited by H. Greeven. Translated by M. Ling. London: SCM/New York: Charles Scribner's Sons, 1956. Original title: "Paulus in Athen." Pp. 71–75 in *Aufsätze zur Apostelgeschichte*. FRLANT 60. Göttingen: Vandenhoeck & Ruprecht, 1951. Second edition: 1953.

   Paul's speech to the Athenians on the Aereopagus gives insight into the Lukan understanding of tailoring the Christian sermon to cultured Gentiles. "The true parallels to this speech are found not in Paul but in Cicero and Seneca and their predecessors" (p. 82).

470 M. Dibelius. "Paul in the Acts of the Apostles." Pp. 207–14 in *Studies in the Acts of the Apostles*. Edited by H. Greeven. Translated by M. Ling. London: SCM/New York: Charles Scribner's Sons, 1956. Original title: "Paulus in der Apostelgeschichte." Pp. 175–80 in *Aufsätze zur Apostelgeschichte*. FRLANT 60. Göttingen: Vandenhoeck & Ruprecht, 1951. Second edition: 1953.

Studies the four major complexes of stories and speeches in Acts which tell the story of Paul to highlight Luke's editorial purposes.

471 A. N. Sherwin-White. *Roman Society and Roman Law in the New Testament*, pp. 48–193. Oxford: Oxford University Press, 1963. Reprinted Grand Rapids: Baker, 1978.

Classic study of Luke's portrayal of Paul in relation to Roman law and society—e.g., Roman jurisprudence, citizenship, civic government, etc.

472 G. Bornkamm. "The Missionary Stance of Paul in I Corinthians 9 and in Acts." Pp. 194–207 in *Studies in Luke-Acts* (P. Schubert Festschrift). Edited by L. E. Keck and J. L. Martyn. Nashville: Abingdon, 1966.

A brief exposition of 1 Corinthians 9:19–23 and its comparison with passages in Acts which shed light on Paul's missionary strategy "to illustrate Paul's phrase that he became to the Jews like a Jew, to those under the law like one under the law (I Cor. 9:20)" (p. 194).

473 J. Knox. "Acts and the Pauline Letter Corpus." Pp. 279–87 in *Studies in Luke-Acts* (P. Schubert Festschrift). Edited by L. E. Keck and J. L. Martyn. Nashville: Abingdon, 1966.

The composition of Acts, subsequent to the publication of the Pauline letter corpus, was prompted by their schismatic use by pre-Marcionite or Marcionite Christians. Luke has intentionally down-played the letter-writing activities of the Pauline mission because of this fact.

474 P. Borgen. "From Paul to Luke: Observations toward Clarification of the Theology of Luke-Acts." *CBQ* 31 (1969): 168–82. Reprinted in Borgen's *Paul Preaches Circumcision and Pleases Men and Other Essays on Christian Origins*, pp. 43–57. Trondheim: Tapir, 1983.

From a study of Romans 9–11, 15, and 1 Corinthians
15:1–11, Borgen presents a nuanced reassessment, *contra*
P. Vielhauer (#468), of the relationship between Lukan
and Pauline theology regarding: Luke's dependence on
Paul, the dependence of both on primitive tradition, the
Jewish rejection of the gospel, the time of the Gentiles as
an interim period, and the alleged influence of the delay
of the parousia.

475 C. K. Barrett. "The Acts—of Paul." Pp. 86–100 in *New Testament Essays*. London: SPCK, 1972.

In dialog with P. Vielhauer (#468), E. Haenchen (#29),
H. Conzelmann (#37), and others, concludes that the
Paulinisms of Acts are not a corruption of Pauline theology as much as they are a pastoral development and application to a new historical situation, though lacking Paul's
profundity.

476 F. F. Bruce. "Is the Paul of Acts the Real Paul?" *BJRL* 58
(1975–76): 282–305.

Argues that Acts truly reflects the biography and theology of Paul as seen in retrospect through the eyes of a
friend and admirer, yet writing for another audience and
purpose.

477 C. K. Barrett. "Acts and the Pauline Corpus." *ExpTim* 88
(1976): 2–5.

Asserts that Luke, who belonged to a non-Pauline stream
of Christianity, did not know Paul's letters; Luke's account of Paul reflects Luke's Gentile theology.

478 F. F. Bruce. "Paul and the Athenians." *ExpTim* 88 (1976): 8–
12.

Concludes that Paul in Acts 17:22–31 presents the theology of Romans 1–3 adapted to a pagan audience. Paul does
not argue from the first principles of Greek philosophy
but bases his message on biblical revelation and Old Testament thought and language.

479 R. Jeske. "Luke and Paul on the Apostle Paul." *CTM* 4
(1977): 28–38.

A summary and chronology of Paul's life based on the principle that Acts is a useful source where it is in accord with or harmoniously supplements the Pauline data.

480 A. J. Mattill Jr. "The Value of Acts as a Source for the Study of Paul." Pp. 76–98 in *Perspectives on Luke-Acts.* Edited by C. H. Talbert. Danville, Va.: Association of Baptist Professors of Religion/Edinburgh: T. & T. Clark, 1978.

Surveys the history of criticism on this topic from the perspectives of the major schools, outlining their basic positions, methodologies, conclusions, and relative strengths.

481 R. F. O'Toole. "Luke's Notion of 'Be Imitators of Me as I am of Christ' in Acts 25–26." *BTB* 8 (1978): 155–61.

Explores how, though Luke often expresses his theology differently than Paul, Luke's account of Paul pictures how Paul lives out his own command in 1 Corinthians 11:1.

482 C. J. A. Hickling. "The Portrait of Paul in Acts 26." Pp. 499–503 in *Les Actes des Apôtres: Traditions, Rédaction, Théologie.* Edited by J. Kremer. BETL 48. Leuven: Leuven University Press, 1979.

Suggests that, in relation to the depiction of Paul as wonder worker in chapters 13–19, "the Paul of chapters 21–26 is a figure intended not so much to recapitulate as to supplement, or even to correct the undesirable implications of, the earlier, more popular narratives" (pp. 502–3). Moreover, "the dramatic qualities of the narrative of the trials are an essential part of the technique by which his character is presented; and . . . these dramatic qualities appear at their highest peak in the speech before Agrippa and its sequel" (p. 503).

483 J. Jervell. "Paul in the Acts of the Apostles: Tradition, History, Theology." Pp. 297–306 in *Les Actes des Apôtres: Traditions, Rédaction, Théologie.* Edited by J. Kremer. BETL 48. Leuven: Leuven University Press, 1979. Reprinted in Jervell's *The Unknown Paul: Essays on Luke-Acts and Early Christian History,* pp. 68–76. Minneapolis: Augsburg, 1984.

On two important aspects of Luke's portrayal of Paul—
namely, the enduring Jewishness of Paul and Paul the vi-
sionary and miracle worker—what Luke presents is historically accurate even if it is not the whole of Paul.

484 J. Jervell. "The Signs of an Apostle: Paul's Miracles." Translated by R. A. Harrisville. Pp. 79–95 in *The Unknown Paul:
Essays on Luke-Acts and Early Christian History.* Minneapolis: Augsburg, 1984. Original title: "Die Zeichen des Apos-
tels: Die Wunder beim lukanischen und paulinischen Paulus." *Studien zum Neuen Testament und seiner Umwelt* 5
(1980): 54–75.

A comparison of the performance and understanding of
Paul's miracles in Acts and the letters of Paul in relation
to word, apostolic office, Spirit, and weakness.

485 M. Black. "Paul and Roman Law in Acts." *Restoration
Quarterly* 24 (1981): 209–18.

Considers Paul's treatment in Acts as an accurate portrayal of provincial Roman law in regard to what was
known of Roman citizenship in ancient sources.

486 S. M. Praeder. "Miracle Worker and Missionary: Paul in the
Acts of the Apostles." Pp. 107–29 in *Society of Biblical Lit-
erature 1983 Seminar Papers.* Edited by K. H. Richards.
Chico, Calif.: Scholars Press, 1983.

Literary study of Paul's miracles, as well as Jesus-Paul
and Peter-Paul parallels, in relation to Paul's role as missionary and their development of theological themes in
Luke-Acts.

487 R. L. Brawley. "Paul in Acts: Lucan Apology and Conciliation." Pp. 129–47 in *Luke-Acts: New Perspectives from the
Society of Biblical Literature Seminar.* Edited by C. H. Talbert. New York: Crossroad, 1984.

By examining Paul's Gentile mission, parallel legitimation techniques in Hellenistic literature, and identifying
traces of anti-Pauline opponents in Acts, contends that
Luke's portrait of Paul is both irenic and apologetic.

488 G. W. Trompf. "On Why Luke Declined to Recount the
Death of Paul: Acts 27–28 and Beyond." Pp. 225–39 in *Luke-
Acts: New Perspectives from the Society of Biblical Litera-*

ture Seminar. Edited by C. H. Talbert. New York: Cross-road, 1984.

Luke ends his second volume before disclosing Paul's fate, quite possibly his beheading, because it did not suit his artistic, political, and historico-theological intentions—most notably his theme of divine retribution.

489 B. R. Gaventa. "The Overthrown Enemy: Luke's Portrait of Paul." Pp. 439–49 in *Society of Biblical Literature 1985 Seminar Papers.* Edited by K. H. Richards. Atlanta: Scholars Press, 1985.

Luke's repetition of Paul's conversion signifies its importance in Acts. Though the methodological question of approaching these passages remains problematic, Gaventa asserts that Luke tailors each account to its context, Paul's conversion is characterized as "the enemy that is overthrown," and Paul's conversion narratives must contribute to an understanding of the Lukan Paul.

490 E. Larsson. "Paul: Law and Salvation." *NTS* 31 (1985): 425–36.

After contrasting Paul's view of the law in Acts and the Epistles, calls into question the ability to investigate Paul's view of the law from a redaction-history perspective because of the constraints of Luke's historical circumstances. Nevertheless, it is asserted that Acts may in fact preserve historical traits of Paul which his polemical letters do not disclose.

491 P. B. Mather. "Paul in Acts as 'Servant' and 'Witness.'" *Biblical Research* 30 (1985): 23–44.

Luke has developed his portrayal of Paul as servant and witness through the correspondence of Acts 6–9 and 22–23 in the same way he has developed the correspondence of Luke 9 and 22–23.

492 W. O. Walker. "Acts and the Pauline Corpus Reconsidered." *JSNT* 24 (1985): 3–23.

In writing Acts, Luke knew and used some of Paul's letters, though never mentioning them. Because of the abuse of Paul's writings by sectarians, Acts may have been shaped as an introduction to Paul's letters to reclaim him for mainstream Christianity.

493 M. D. Goulder. "Did Luke Know Any of the Pauline Letters?" *PRS* 13 (1986): 97–112.

Charts the verbal and conceptual parallels between Acts and Paul's letters to the Corinthians and Thessalonians, contending that Luke knew these letters and may have settled near Corinth after Paul's death.

494 F. F. Bruce. "Paul's Use of the Old Testament in Acts." Pp. 71–79 in *Tradition and Interpretation in the New Testament: Essays in Honor of E. Earle Ellis for His 60th Birthday*. Edited by G. F. Hawthorne and O. Betz. Grand Rapids: Eerdmans/Tübingen: Mohr, 1987.

A brief survey of Paul's use of the Old Testament in his speeches in Acts, leading to the conclusion that Paul's Old Testament quotations are Lukan in composition but "reproduce the total purport of what was actually said" (p. 77).

495 D. J. Lull (ed.). *Society of Biblical Literature 1988 Seminar Papers*, pp. 82–131. Atlanta: Scholars Press, 1988.

Four papers on the Paulinism of Acts, including work by J. A. Fitzmyer, R. Brawley, J. T. Carroll, and J. Townsend.

496 D. Wenham. "The Paulinism of Acts Again." *Themelios* 13 (1988): 53–55.

A comparison of selected passages in Acts with 1 Thessalonians 1:9–10 and 5:12–13 suggests the accuracy of Luke's information concerning Paul's evangelistic ministry and appointment of elders.

497 S. Dockx. "The First Missionary Voyage of Paul: Historical Reality or Literary Creation of Luke?" Pp. 209–21 in *Chronos, Kairos, Christos: Nativity and Chronological Studies Presented to Jack Finegan*. Edited by J. Vardaman and E. M. Yamauchi. Winona Lake: Eisenbrauns, 1989.

Study of the chronological problems raised concerning Paul's ascent(s) to Jerusalem as recorded in Acts and Galatians, concluding that the Lukan account is in fact a literary creation.

498 I. H. Marshall. "Luke's View of Paul." *Southwest Journal of Theology* 33 (1990): 41–51.

Examines Luke's portrayal of Paul's mission, natural theology, christology, eschatology, and view of the Law in Acts; denying the assumption that Luke misrepresented, was misinformed concerning, or did not know Paul.

499 R. I. Pervo. *Luke's Story of Paul.* Minneapolis: Fortress, 1990.

Luke's portrayal of Paul in Acts is facilitated by attention to the narrative's plot in an attempt "to present the story in its freshness and assist each reader to approach Acts with the naiveté of a 'first reader,' one who does not know how the story will turn out" (p. 13).

500 D. Schwartz. "The End of the Line: Paul in the Canonical Book of Acts." Pp. 3–24 in *Paul and the Legacies of Paul.* Edited by W. S. Babcock. Dallas: Southern Methodist University Press, 1990.

Paulinisms in Acts evince Luke's concern with telling a story rather than developing personalities; the characters have a role to play in the larger story of Luke-Acts, not their own story.

501 J. C. Lentz. *Luke's Portrait of Paul.* SNTSMS 77. Cambridge: Cambridge University Press, 1993.

"The careful reader of Acts should be confounded by the way St. Paul is portrayed" (p. 1) since, it is argued, Paul the strict Pharisee would not likely have held or been proud of Roman citizenship. The high social status and exemplary moral virtue attributed to Paul in Acts is a Lukan fiction aimed at winning high-ranking citizens of the Empire to the Christian faith.

502 B. M. Rapske. "The Lukan Defense of the Missionary Prisoner Paul." *TynB* 44 (1993): 193–96.

Abstracts Rapske's "Pauline Imprisonment and the Lukan Defense of the Missionary Prisoner Paul in the Light of Greco-Roman Sources" (Ph.D. diss., University of Aberdeen, 1992). Asserts that Luke was concerned to show, despite the highly negative stigma Paul would have carried as a result of his frequent and lengthy imprisonment, that he was nonetheless (1) an effective missionary, (2) the recipient of assistance from Christians and other persons, and (3) approved by God.

503 M.-E. Rosenblatt. *Paul the Accused: His Portrait in the Acts of the Apostles*. Zacchaeus Studies: New Testament. Collegeville, Minn.: Liturgical, 1994.

Paul is not Luke's vehicle for carrying his opinion of the Roman government, whether positive or negative, but rather serves as a model for Christians who, in the course of the church's mission, face struggles similar to those Paul encountered.

10.3.6 The "We Passages" in Acts

Apart from the prefaces of the Third Gospel and Acts (see §4.1), Luke consistently maintains a position as narrator *outside* of the account. In Acts 16:10–17; 20:5–21:17; and chapters 27–28, however, he adopts a perspective from *within* the story. How is this to be explained? Discussion of the phenomenon of the Lukan narrator's shift from third to first person in the "we passages" of Acts typically centers around the following: Luke as a participant in these historical events mentioned in the last half of Acts; a change in Luke's source at these points; the presence of a Hellenistic literary convention; or an overriding literary/theological concern on Luke's part.

504 M. Dibelius. "The Acts of the Apostles in the Setting of the History of Early Christian Literature" (esp. pp. 201–6). Pp. 192–206 in *Studies in the Acts of the Apostles*. Edited by H. Greeven. Translated by M. Ling. London: SCM/New York: Charles Scribner's Sons, 1956. Original title: "Die Apostelgeschichte in Rahmen der urchristlichen Literaturgeschichte." Pp. 163–74 in *Aufsätze zur Apostelgeschichte*. FRLANT 60. Göttingen: Vandenhoeck & Ruprecht, 1951. Second edition: 1953.

Includes examples of Greco-Roman, Jewish, and Christian literature which employ an analogous "we style," as well as a discussion of its "distinctly literary" use in Acts.

505 H. J. Cadbury. "'We' and 'I' Passages in Luke-Acts." *NTS* 3 (1956–57): 128–32.

Concludes, from an examination of the endings of the "we passages" and the prologue to the Gospel, that the author is claiming personal participation in Acts as a whole or at least in its latter part. This prepares the reader for the occurrence of the first person plural in these passages.

506 E. Haenchen. "'We' in Acts and the Itinerary." *Journal for Theology and Church* 1 (1965): 65–99. Original title: "Dar 'Wir' in der Apostelgeshichte und das Itinerar." *Zeitschrift für Theologie und Kirche* 58 (1961): 329–66.

Concludes that the "we passages" are the work of the author drawing upon various sources rather than extracts from a travel itinerary, that the use of the first person plural serves Luke's historical and rhetorical purposes, and that this literary device is used economically so that *historiography* does not become *novel*.

507 V. K. Robbins. "The We-Passages in Acts and Ancient Sea Voyages." *Biblical Research* 20 (1975): 5–18.

Investigates the narrative use of first and third person in Hellenistic literature and their parallels in Acts, suggesting that Luke has drawn upon a generic feature of ancient sea-voyage narratives in the "we passages."

508 A. J. Mattill Jr. "The Value of Acts as a Source for the Study of Paul." Pp. 76–98 in *Perspectives on Luke-Acts*. Edited by C. H. Talbert. Danville, Va.: Association of Baptist Professors of Religion/Edinburgh: T. & T. Clark, 1978.

Surveys the history of criticism on this topic from the perspectives of the major schools, with a concluding emphasis on the critical role that the "we passages" play in each school.

509 V. K. Robbins. "By Land and by Sea: The We-Passages and Ancient Sea Voyages." Pp. 215–42 in *Perspectives on Luke-Acts*. Edited by C. H. Talbert. Danville, Va.: Association of Baptist Professors of Religion/Edinburgh: T. & T. Clark, 1978.

An exploration of Luke's "we passages" as examples of the Hellenistic sea-voyage genre and their function in the structure of Luke-Acts. "This style contributes directly to the author's scheme of participation in history through narration of its dramatic episodes" (p. 217).

510 S. M. Praeder. "Acts 27:1–28:16: Sea Voyages in Ancient Literature and the Theology of Luke-Acts." *CBQ* 46 (1984): 683–706.

Comparative literary and theological study of the relation of the Lukan "we passages" to sea-voyages in ancient literature and to the theology of Luke-Acts, emphasizing the internal literary connections and the theological theme of sending salvation to the Gentiles.

511 C. J. Hemer. "First Person Narrative in Acts 27–28." *TynB* 36 (1985): 79–109.

Argues, *contra* V. K. Robbins (#509), that use of the first person plural is not characteristic of the Hellenistic sea-voyage genre. Rather, extra-biblical texts imply Luke's personal participation in the account of Acts 27–28.

512 R. C. Tannehill. *The Narrative Unity of Luke-Acts: A Literary Interpretation*, Vol. 2: *The Acts of the Apostles*, pp. 246–47, 264, 330. Foundations and Facets. Philadelphia: Fortress, 1986.

Underscores the literary functions of the "we passages" as a focalizing character: "The anonymous 'we'—a participant narrator—is a special opportunity for us and others to enter the narrative as participants and to see ourselves as companions of Paul as he prepares the churches for his absence and resolutely approaches the danger in Jerusalem" (p. 247); as a non-omniscient narrator who shares the limited insight of Paul's companions (cf. Acts 21:1–16); and as a symbol of the extension of community subsequent to Paul's breaking bread (cf. Acts 27:33–38) where the "we" shifts from the small number of Christians to include the entire ship's company.

513 W. S. Kurz. "Narrative Approaches to Luke-Acts." *Biblica* 68 (1987): 195–220 (esp. pp. 204–20).

The assertion that narrative approaches may function as supplemental to historical and tradition-critical readings of Luke-Acts is illustrated in the treatment of the "we passages." After a critique of V. Robbins' (#509) treatment, Kurz concludes, "In terms of the plot, the narrator's presence on some of Paul's journeys and absence in his trials is much like Peter's presence and absence during Jesus' journeys and trials" (p. 219).

514 R. I. Pervo. *Profit with Delight: The Literary Genre of the Acts of the Apostles*, pp. 50–57. Philadelphia: Fortress, 1987.

Argues, *contra* S. Praeder and akin to V. Robbins (#509), that the "we passages" are examples of a fixed Greek convention. Demonstrates, moreover, the heightened literary quality of Acts 27, that shipwreck and travel accounts were a staple of ancient adventures rather than novels, and concludes with an excursion on the "itinerary style."

515 S. M. Praeder. "The Problem of First-Person Narration in Acts." *NovT* 29 (1987): 193–218.

A review of scholarship on first-person narration in Acts, concluding that several aspects of this problem remain unexplained and can only be addressed by drawing upon diverse methodologies.

516 J. A. Fitzmyer. "The Authorship of Luke-Acts Reconsidered." Pp. 1–26 in *Luke the Theologian: Aspects of His Teaching*. New York/Mahwah: Paulist, 1989.

A rearticulation of the position which posits Luke, the sometime companion of Paul, as the author of Luke-Acts, based on second century C.E. traditions, the Epistle to the Philippians and Luke's presence in Philippi and Macedonia, and a critique of V. K. Robbins' (#509) theory of the literary character of the "we-sections."

517 C. J. Hemer. *The Book of Acts in the Setting of Hellenistic History*, pp. 308–34. WUNT 49. Edited by C. H. Gempf. Tübingen: Mohr, 1989.

Within a larger analysis of Paul's chronology and the authorship and sources of Acts, asserts Luke's personal participation as the most reasonable explanation for the "we passages."

Index to Modern Authors